"Behind every story of redemption in God's kingdom is some kind of story of prayer. Dawes is not just offering a kind of theology of prayer that is simple and easy. Rather, he is subversively giving us a way to experience redemption. Eat this book. Slowly. Like dark chocolate. It very well may open up an entirely new story for redemption in your life."
A. J. Swoboda, Fuller Theological Seminary, author of *The Dusty Ones*

"There are those books you read when the timing is just right and the words on a page are more Technicolor than black and white. Every once in a while, a book intersects your theology, your praxis, and our culture at exactly the right moment to produce catalytic growth and deep transformation. *Simple Prayer* is such a book. If you're tired, worn out, and burned out on religion, this book invites you to a new, ancient way of connecting with the triune God."
April L. Diaz, leadership coach, speaker, author

"Charlie Dawes is restless and ready to walk the more difficult path, if that's what it takes to follow Jesus. And yet his is a simple spirituality—one that begins with 'breathe in, breathe out' and the simple prayers that follow. The words that form his prayers are expertly woven throughout his story. Charlie is an avid storyteller—one whose readers are delighted upon finding their own story and prayer within his pages."
Donna K. Wallace, *New York Times*–bestselling author

"In *Simple Prayer*, we encounter a young man groaning for a deeper connection to God—a connection not to be gained by jettisoning his heritage among the charismatics, but one that will deepen what he already knows. Charlie Dawes discovered a simple prayer in the deepest pockets of the Christian tradition, and this led him to look for other simple prayers throughout the Scriptures. To read this book is to be challenged to go deeper with God through the simplest of prayers."
Scot McKnight, professor of New Testament, Northern Seminary, author of *The Jesus Creed*

"I've seen Charlie Dawes in many roles. Son, husband, father. Speaker, pastor, worship leader. Professor, writer, friend. In each position he functions with a creative mind and a compassionate spirit. His words can invite others into a world of Christlikeness in any area. Don't miss the chance to learn from a man who has chosen to continue learning daily in every area of life."
Chris Maxwell, campus pastor, Emmanuel College, author of *Underwater*

"We live in a time when a generation is fixated on being consistently connected through the Internet. It's refreshing to read a book so well written about our connection with our Creator. I believe this book will encourage people to see prayer not as a chore but as a choice—a choice that enables us to have that intimate relationship with God that he designed us for."

Dan Blythe, pastor, Hillsong Church UK

"*Simple Prayer* has an authenticity, specificity, and electricity that is incandescent. Dawes shows how simplicity of prayer is the ultimate maturity of faith and sophistication of soul."

Leonard Sweet, professor, Drew University, George Fox University,
Tabor College, author, founder of Preachthestory.com

"Prayer is the forefront of the spiritual life and essential to our development as disciples, yet practicing prayer is overcomplicated more often than not. *Simple Prayer* brings us back to the basics, encouraging us to make prayer a matter of the heart. This book paves the way for you to know and be known by God."

Stovall Weems, senior pastor, Celebration Church

"This is a must-read on how to make prayer more personal and powerful. *Simple Prayer* is as practical as it is challenging, with Charlie Dawes ending each chapter actually putting simple prayers into practice. As the reader, you quickly come to realize that this is not just another book on prayer, but rather a book that leads you in prayer. You will marvel at how much more meaningful your prayer life can become."

Kent Ingle, president, Southeastern University, Lakeland, Florida,
author of *This Adventure Called Life, 9 Disciplines of Enduring Leadership,*
and *Framework Leadership*

simple prayer

LEARNING TO

SPEAK TO GOD

WITH EASE

Charlie Dawes

Foreword by Mark Batterson

IVP Books

An imprint of InterVarsity Press
Downers Grove, Illinois

InterVarsity Press
P.O. Box 1400, Downers Grove, IL 60515-1426
ivpress.com
email@ivpress.com

InterVarsity Press® is the book-publishing division of InterVarsity Christian Fellowship/USA®, a movement of students and faculty active on campus at hundreds of universities, colleges, and schools of nursing in the United States of America, and a member movement of the International Fellowship of Evangelical Students. For information about local and regional activities, visit intervarsity.org.

While any stories in this book are true, some names and identifying information may have been changed to protect the privacy of individuals.

Published in association with the literary agency of Mark Oestreicher.

Cover design: Cindy Kiple
Interior design: Daniel van Loon
Images: © mhatzapa/iStockphoto

ISBN 978-0-8308-4481-4 (print)
ISBN 978-0-8308-8107-9 (digital)

Printed in the United States of America ♾

Library of Congress Cataloging-in-Publication Data

Names: Dawes, Charlie, author.
Title: Simple prayer : learning to speak to God with ease / Charlie Dawes ; foreword by Mark Batterson.
Description: Downers Grove : InterVarsity Press, 2017. | Includes bibliographical references.
Identifiers: LCCN 2017022346 (print) | LCCN 2017019789 (ebook) | ISBN 9780830881079 (eBook) | ISBN 9780830844814 (pbk. : alk. paper)
Subjects: LCSH: Prayer--Christianity.
Classification: LCC BV210.3 (print) | LCC BV210.3 .D39 2017 (ebook) | DDC 248.3/2--dc23
LC record available at https://lccn.loc.gov/2017022346

P   25   24   23   22   21   20   19   18   17   16   15   14   13   12   11   10   9   8   7   6   5   4   3   2   1

Y   36   35   34   33   32   31   30   29   28   27   26   25   24   23   22   21   20   19   18   17

For Nicole:

Deep down I am still the teenage boy

hoping this impresses you.

You make life far greater than any dream.

Contents

Foreword

Mark Batterson

Prayer can sometimes be a frightening thing. How do we approach the Maker of the world? It begins by viewing prayer as a deeper experience than simply trying to elicit a response from God. It is natural to go to God when we need something, but how much more would our lives change if we had prayer as a natural rhythm and practice in our lives?

In *Simple Prayer*, Charlie Dawes offers readers an opportunity to simplify their prayer life and in doing so, make it richer. Charlie has a strong passion to help people on their spiritual journey; he thrives on mentoring, teaching, and discipling, and this is evident to those around him. His love of people and pop culture makes his voice a unique and fresh connection between age-old wisdom and the twenty-first century.

This book will open the door for you to experience the same presence of God that you may feel during worship in your everyday life. It is never too late to become a person of prayer. It's simple, straightforward, challenging, and hopeful. Charlie uses simple prayers to create a personal connection to God for all denominations.

Prayer has been a central part of the Christian life for centuries and yet remains a point of anxiety for many. Prayer can feel difficult and burdensome, and Charlie offers a reminder that sometimes the most powerful prayers are the ones that are simple in nature. It was his discovery of the ancient prayer known as the Jesus Prayer that introduced Charlie to a new rhythm of prayer. It was one that was focused on being with God more than talking to God. This knowledge from the past can be and is personal for today! *Simple Prayer* offers prayers that will be foundational in your prayer life, ministry, and relationships.

I challenge you to let this book change how you pray. Prayer is more than a list. It's not a stale transaction between you and God—prayer is an intimate part of your spirituality. Simple prayers are the catalyst you need for spiritual depth. This book is an invitation to allow simple prayers to shape your spiritual practice of prayer and to be the start of a beautiful journey in spiritual formation.

Introduction

Let's begin a book on prayer in a bar.

The roaring twenties were marked by brilliant jazz musicians and new forms of dancing. Women made significant gains in the workplace, and the female voice was for the first time being heard on ballots. The country's citizens were connected to one another, and innovation was launching them into new terrain. City life was becoming a focal point, with the farm fading in the rearview mirror of the Model T. And on January 16, 1920, the federal Volstead Act closed every tavern, bar, and saloon in the country. Most likely, that same day the speakeasy was birthed. When people across the country found their favorite bars closed, they sought to create an alternate reality for the consumption of their favorite libations.

The original speakeasies were places filled with excitement and exclusion. To gain entrance to the club, you would approach the unmarked door and knock twice, and then a small peephole would slide open just wide enough for a pair of eyes to appear and prompt you for the password. The right word granted you entrance into a brand-new world, and the wrong word left you in the alley only able to hear the faint whisper of the roaring jazz music dancing in the damp night air.

The quest for a deeper spiritual life has often left me on the outside looking in. I grew up in church and have heard more sermons than I can count. The songs of the church filled my family's home while we sang our theology in three-part harmony. I have heard stories of God's faithfulness and nearness for as long as I can remember—yet I found myself without the right password to gain entrance. All of the talk about a deeper walk, a more powerful prayer life, left me feeling like the church was a spiritual speakeasy that housed the music, community, and the Spirit. It promised everything I wanted, but I didn't have the password to gain entry.

When Jesus speaks of the kingdom he does so with childlike simplicity, and yet I was finding it more and more difficult to feel like I was a part. If you have ever felt like going deeper in your relationship with Jesus is just beyond your grasp, keep reading. If you have ever wanted to find the right words to guide you to God, this book is for you. If you have ever wanted it to not be so difficult, it's simpler than you've been told.

WHAT IS SIMPLE PRAYER?

The word *simple* means not hard to understand, not complex or fancy. Simple prayer acknowledges who I am in light of who God is and leaves no need for many words. Often when I don't know what to say I say too much. Proverbs says that when words are in excess, sin isn't absent (Proverbs 10:19). Many words or complex thoughts do not equal nearness to God. The role of prayer in our lives is like the facets on a diamond—many angles and new brilliance are displayed at each turn. Prayer aligns us with God, and our thinking is renewed in light of that connection. Simple prayer strips away the dross that fills our speech and gives us a direct connection to God. It is not less prayer—it is indeed more. Simple prayer is a way of praying that keeps the focus of our prayers in clear view. This model of prayer is at once accessible to someone exploring spirituality and provides plenty of depth for the seasoned Christ-follower.

The life of simple prayer is a prayerful life that unfolds behind the scenes, often unheard. It is a way to recalibrate your prayer life and bring renewal when prayers become focused on everything but God alone. The beauty in prayer comes when the desire to be with God is greater than the desire to get things from God, when our word count is less important than the language we use.

This book will introduce simple prayer in a way that invites you to practice what you are reading. A book on prayer is less effective than a book that leads you in prayer, and planning times of prayer as you read this book will help you take to heart this practice that has been so life changing for me.

WHY IS SIMPLE PRAYER IMPORTANT?

Prayer is at the forefront of the spiritual life and is essential to our development as disciples. Prayer is found throughout the Bible, yet it remains difficult for most of us. We want to pray, but don't know how. We long for depth in our spiritual lives, but aren't sure how to launch out into the deep. Most of us can remember who taught us how to ride a bike or throw a baseball, but can we name the person who taught us to pray? If we are pushed on the matter, we realize that we likely weren't taught *how* to pray but rather were told *about* prayer.

Simple prayers have been an important part of my spirituality, providing a means of prayer in times when it was difficult to pray. They have also invited me to strip away all the meaningless words with which I tend to fill my prayers so I can get down to the heart of prayer—being with God. By introducing me to a prayer life that is sustainable and accessible, simple prayers have made all the difference in my life.

Simple prayers are important to help form our prayer lives and allow us to create rhythms in our inner lives that we can build on. Simple prayers keep us moving toward God. They create a foundation on which the rest of our prayers stand. They provide places to start or places to return.

Simple prayers have been prayed for centuries. We find them throughout the Scriptures and scattered throughout our lives—in songs and literature, in conversations about God, in conversations with our kids. A practice of simple prayer gives us the opportunity to pick up these gems, dust them off, and begin to pray the way Jesus prayed, the way he taught the disciples, and the way countless other followers of Jesus have prayed throughout the centuries.

PRAYERS FILLED WITH PURPOSE

Simple prayers are not lazy prayers; they are purposed prayers. Simple prayer is not getting out of prayer or reducing our experience; it is becoming deliberate in our language regarding the things that matter. I have a deep desire to make my words count. I want to carefully choose words that paint a picture and capture emotions or thought, but I also want to do that in a way that is most accessible and effective. A good poet knows that the right word is better than ten almost right words. These right words aren't hidden; they are scattered all around for us to find. Simple prayer reminds us that prayer isn't for those with access to secret places or pedigree but for all of us.

Prayer has many facets, and simple prayer is one of them. The biblical call to prayer without ceasing is better translated, "Come to rest." Prayer is a restful and reflective activity. Prayer is being present to God and being renewed and reformed in his image. It is part dialogue and part enjoyment of being with him. It is deep breaths of refreshing and passionate cries from our hearts. Simple prayers are not void of emotion; they are calculated and focused emotion: say-what-we-mean-and-mean-what-we-say types of prayers. If we are not careful, our prayer lives will look more like the pagan worship in the Old Testament, when people were certain the gods heard them based on their expressive language and rituals. In contrast, Jesus taught us to pray in a way that is honest, heartfelt, and simple.

PRAYING LIKE YOU MEAN IT

In the summer of 1998, I became the youth pastor at the church in which I grew up, situated in the shadows of Disney World and Universal Studios in central Florida. I remember my first day quite clearly. My heart was brimming with excitement, and enthusiasm was seeping out of the corners of my smile. I marched up the sidewalk to the outside office door, extended my hand to greet the doorknob, and with a deep breath turned the handle and entered the office.

My pastor had been a mentor and friend for years. Now we were working together, and he was as excited as I was. He had a smile as big as mine. He looked me right in the eye and asked, "Are you ready to get to work?"

Truth be told, I had no idea what that meant or what I was getting myself into, but without hesitation I exclaimed, "Yes!"

He replied, "Follow me." He walked to the door that led to the sanctuary, opened the door, and disappeared.

Before the door fully closed, I slid through and entered a few steps behind him. He walked off the stage and down two more steps to the altar area. "Charlie, I am excited for you to work here. Now here is your first lesson in ministry. Work begins in here, in prayer before anything else. The rest can wait. The phones will ring and mail will be delivered, but first things first. We pray." He turned to the left and began to walk the room and pray. His walk wasn't a march; it was a stroll. He wasn't in a hurry or on a mission. He was going somewhere, but nowhere near where we were. If you looked closely you could see the familiar path of his footsteps impressed on the faded blue carpet. I just knelt down at the altar and began to pray.

I prayed for everything that I could think of. I prayed for family members to be saved, I prayed for every friend and world leader I could recall. I prayed for world peace and for hunger to be quenched throughout the earth. I believed that because of my passion and it being my first day on the job, God would be inclined to respond as I requested. I was certain that due to the intensity of my prayer drops of blood were forming on my head, so I patted my head with the end of my shirt. I looked at my watch to see how much time had passed. To my surprise, it had only been ten minutes. I turned my head to see how my pastor was doing, and he smiled at me and kept walking and praying. Feeling inadequate, I turned from my kneeling position to sitting on the floor with my back leaning against the altar, and I began to listen.

At that time, I wasn't aware of the instruction that I was receiving from my pastor. I was learning what it meant to be a person who prayed. His prayers were not filled with vernacular that was impossible to understand. They were simple words, simple phrases. Simple prayers might have been whispered from his lips, but they roared in heaven. I sat clinging to every word. I began to repeat them softly as if they were my own. That was the first day that I allowed another person's prayers to be my own. The words didn't lose meaning when I borrowed them; they grew stronger in my heart. They became my own. I didn't learn any techniques or tricks of the trade that day. We didn't dialogue about ministry philosophy or the mission, vision, and values of the church. We prayed simple prayers.

PRAYER FOR WHEREVER YOU ARE

As we launch into the rest of this book, the goal is to provide you with a collection of simple prayers to interact with and make your own. They come from places far and wide and give the reader an entry into a life of prayer that is simple but not simplistic. The purpose of simple prayer is to find our hearts closer and more connected to God. Prayer is the vehicle that brings us to the Father, and it is prayer that creates space for us to settle in. This book is for those desiring to live a life of prayer that is not disjointed.

Simple prayers are all around us. They are found in Scripture. They are hidden in our daily lives. They swirl around our hearts and minds and rest on the tips of our tongues. Simple prayers are for both the novice seeker and the well-worn traveler on the journey of faith. Where do you find yourself at this moment? Are you new to faith? Have you been on this faith walk for years? Do you feel like you are losing your way? Do you feel the wind at your back propelling you into unchartered waters and have a rising anxiety about the unknown? Maybe you are looking for a way to deepen your prayer life. Then it is time to simply pray. We can trust that before we even articulate our thoughts, emotions, or needs, God already knows and desires to respond. A simple prayer paves the way for us to know and be known by God.

This book is for those too busy to pray and for those who have found their prayers to be lifeless. This is a chance to connect our prayer with historic prayers that have carried believers for centuries, and for those prayers to create space in our inner lives for us to be with God. Perhaps what we need are fewer books to tell us about prayer and more that help us pray. I hope you will find this book to be the latter.

Let's pray.

1

What Is Simple Prayer?

If you can't explain it simply, you don't understand it well enough.
ALBERT EINSTEIN

I grew up in a house where prayer was a normal part of our daily lives. I can't remember how many times I would wake up for school before the sun peeked out from the covers of night to find my mom sitting in a chair in the living room praying and reading her Bible. Often before heading into the bathroom to shower the slumber away, I would listen; I would learn. I heard her pray for a lot of things, most of them now forgotten, but what I remember are the prayers for me—prayers for protection, prayers to sense the nearness of God throughout the day. It was the simplicity of the phrases that made the impact.

It seemed there was a level of intimacy that did not require an excess of words. To flood the moment with wordiness would almost violate the relationship. When my mom would pray, "Be with him, Lord," it was a prayer filled with vision and hope. It was a prayer immersed in a trust that the Holy Spirit would surround me with protection, provision, and power. God's response to the prayer had nothing to do with the word count but only with the unbridled dependency my mom had on God. Hearing her simple prayers had a profound impact on my life. Little did I know that learning to pray simple prayers would yield large returns in my own spiritual journey.

Simple prayer is a prayer of intimacy and confidence that our prayers give way to the deeper cry of our hearts. Before we can delve into an investigation of simple prayer, we need to make certain of our understanding of what prayer is and what it isn't. This chapter explores the distinctions between simple prayer and many common understandings of prayer, and it suggests ways to launch out into this ancient prayer model to experience a depth in our spirituality.

MISSING THE POINT OF IT ALL

Adventures in Missing the Point is one of my favorite book titles. For me it describes well my personal spiritual journey. Sometimes I have great intentions but miss the target. Prayer has been one of those adventures. I have made prayer transactional, trying to use it to elicit a specific response from God, often for my own gain, and I have been too concerned about my prayer performance.

Prayer shouldn't be seen as a mechanism to get what we want from God; it is an opportunity to recognize that God is present and to respond. Prayer provides the entryway into interaction with a God who is here and now. As you read this, he is with you; when you stop reading this he will still be with you (but don't stop yet; we are just getting started). The power of the incarnational ministry of Jesus is that he is among us.

The Message translation puts it this way: "The Word became flesh and blood, and moved into the neighborhood" (John 1:14 *The Message*). Even with the knowledge that God is near and desires to dwell among us, it is easy to slip into a transactional mode when we pray. We all have needs that are pressing, and we serve a God who is our source and supplier, but if we see prayer primarily though this lens, we trade intimacy for a transaction. The invitation of Jesus is an intimate one. Intimacy says, "Come, be known, and then get to know in exchange." Intimacy promises trust and love abounding. Intimacy is what we crave, but often our prayers seem like a wish list offered for fulfillment.

When a transaction is substituted for intimacy, we are left with things as empty and unsatisfying as the sex industry. At the core of the sex industry are people exchanging and destroying relational intimacy because intimacy is viewed as a commodity for sale. This commodity requires much less investment, but the reward is an altered reality and a veiled experience of love and pleasure. True intimacy is so much greater but requires so much more.

Likewise, rather than seeking intimacy in prayer we are tempted to turn prayer into a performance. On paper this is obviously wrong, but in practice it is much more difficult to root out. So much in life is straightforward but difficult to execute. For me, physical exercise is something that I adopted regularly a year and a half ago, but the greatest challenge to my progress is the simplest thing to identify: cereal. Oh, how I love cereal! I am a convicted cereal killer. I crave a bowl in the afternoon and just before bed, and this bowl will not be filled with anything that the wonderful people at Kashi have created. It will be filled with berries—

crunch berries, that is. I have a deep love for the cereal created for kids. I have watched my health progress elevate when I reduce and eliminate the sugary cereals, but how many times do I return to the forbidden aisle and load the cart with more of the Captain's delicacies? More times than I care to admit. Diet adjustment is simple to identify but not always easy to put into action.

This is what prayer often feels like: easy to define yet challenging to implement. Prayer is critical to the spiritual life, but if you are anything like me, prayer leaves you with stage fright. More often than I want to admit, I find myself grasping for the right lines to deliver as if prayer were some type of performance.

I have to be reminded that prayer isn't a show. I know this cognitively, but somewhere between what I know and how I behave, something is lost. Prayer isn't about putting our personal righteousness on display in order to impress. Nor is our spirituality a museum for people to view our most valuable accomplishments and endeavors. When the disciples press Jesus to teach them how to pray, he offers them these thoughts before offering a rhythm to model their prayers by: "You've seen them in action, I'm sure—'playactors' I call them—treating prayer meeting and street corner alike as a stage, acting compassionate as long as someone is watching, playing to the crowds. They get applause, true, but that's all they get" (Matthew 6:2-3 *The Message*).

GROWING IN INTIMACY

The longer I live, the more I come to find this to be true: just because something is simple doesn't mean it is simplistic. "Love your neighbor as yourself" is a simple command, but our obedience to it is not simplistic. The gospel is offered in a way that allows the unlearned to have complete access and at the same time provides the scholar depths to explore. Simple prayer is an invitation to a prayer life that is focused on being with God. It is being direct and to the point. It is intended to be honest and raw. It is both well-written poetry and fragmented sentences that only make sense to God. When I sit on the couch with my wife, Nicole, who I have known for nearly twenty years, many words are not needed. It is not because we have nothing to say, it is because somewhere deep in our souls we are connected on a level where words are not needed to capture the emotions our hearts communicate. Deep calls unto deep.

I remember being young and Nicole telling me that she loved me. It was exhilarating to hear those words as a teenager and think we were writing the greatest love story ever told. After nearly two decades filled with thousands of moments when those three words—*I love you*—have filled the space between us, she is now communicating something far deeper than those words used to communicate. This depth is not demonstrated by the word count or word choice but by the life that we have lived around that statement. I love you means "We have had some tough days, but I'm still here." I love you means "Thank you for the laughs and for being there in the tears." Sometimes I love you means "Thanks for taking out the trash" and even "I forgive you when you forget." Simple prayer is this type of communion with God. It is allowing the life that we live around our prayers to provide a depth in our prayers.

Simple prayer is accompanied by a desire for a deeper experience in prayer, which comes from a passionate heart that wants to move beyond dialogue about God. The desire to know must move past a rogue thought and into a rhythm of thoughts that desire to know and be known. "Prayers are tools, but with this clarification: prayers are not tools for doing or getting, but for being and becoming," write Eugene Peterson and James Watkins. They go on to add, "Most students of the human condition agree that prayer is basic to our existence. Prayer reaches into the unknown for whatever we sense, deep within us, will provide wholeness, or for what we hope, far off, will bring salvation." What is the outcome of prayer? What are the desired results? We must keep these questions close at hand in any meaningful instruction on prayer.

A Scottish theologian warned that "no one ought to undertake [writing about prayer] who has not spent more toil in the practice of prayer than on its principle." It is one thing to study prayer but another thing to practice prayer. This book is a collection of prayers that are tried and true in my life and in the lives of others. This book serves as an invitation for you to join in. Simon Chan offers this challenge: "Theory is not a substitution for practice; rather, it supports practice inasmuch as it explains the significance of it. Prayer, like everything else about the Christian life, begins with our incorporation into Christ." Christian prayer seeks the ultimate outcome of union with God. Simple prayer is a mechanism for this to take place.

A FAMILIAR SIMPLE PRAYER

One vital aspect of oneness with God is bringing your whole life before him and offering it to him without restraint. Most of us have interacted with the Lord's Prayer, though it has too often become a prayer that is rehearsed rather than a prayer model that helps us pray simply. I have been in worship gatherings where the Lord's Prayer is recited without passion or a tangible faith that the words we are saying are true. Sometimes the number of words we use keeps us from focusing on what we are really saying. Simple prayer focuses on making the words count because our words matter. Simple prayer allows our hearts to be precise and focused while providing a vehicle for our minds to descend into our hearts. We pray in such a way that our prayers become the cadence to which we live.

The Lord's Prayer can be a model for simple prayer. It can provide a template on how a few purposed words can become a powerful prayer. Jesus used this prayer to teach the disciples to pray, and we can use it to pray simply. Take a moment and get reacquainted with the prayer.

> Our Father in heaven,
> hallowed be your name.
> Your kingdom come,
> your will be done,
>> on earth as it is in heaven.
> Give us this day our daily bread,
> and forgive us our debts,
>> as we also have forgiven our debtors.
> And lead us not into temptation,
>> but deliver us from evil.
> For yours is the kingdom and the power and the glory,
>> forever. Amen. [May it be so.]

The danger in our familiarity with the Lord's Prayer is that the prayer loses its potency in our lives because we assume we have matured beyond it. We think that we graduate from the simple things of our faith the further we travel, yet nothing could be further from the truth.

Now let's focus on a phrase and allow that to become a simple prayer: *Your kingdom come.*

This phrase captures the central theme in the Gospels—the coming kingdom of God is being established and experienced in the face of tyrannical rulers. The Lord's Prayer was an eschatological reminder that the power Jesus' followers saw around them was not the ultimate power. This prayer demonstrated that the rhythm of life Jesus' followers found themselves in was not the method of living they should buy into. The words are powerful in the midst of the fuller prayer but also stand alone very nicely.

Close your eyes and begin to recite this phrase over and over. Prayer is not done well when done in a hurry. It is important to not hurry but to relax. With every utterance, allow your mind and heart to grasp each word and give space for a deeper meaning to emerge in your heart. Simple prayer leads us into deeper communion with God.

Simple prayer is similar to the practice of sacred reading or lectio divina. This ancient practice is a wonderful way to read the Scriptures. Readers take a passage of Scripture, and as they read they trust the Spirit of God to illuminate a word or a phrase for them to sit with. In the same way that our reading of the Bible can be diluted by trying to read too much at one time, our prayers can lose their focus when we are trying to say too much and don't leave space for the Spirit to interact with our hearts through our words.

When I pray this simple prayer—"your kingdom come"—my soul reminds me that when I pray the word *your*, I am challenged to trust that God is in control. It is not mine, but yours. The word *kingdom* adjusts my eyes away from the powers that try to distract and dominate to the kingdom that is established in grace and mercy. The final word of this simple prayer, *come*, is a request for God to find his way to us, not to be far off but to come near.

SIMPLER AND DEEPER

A desire for a deeper experience in prayer comes from a heart that is passionate to move beyond dialogue about God or how to get what we want from God. The desire to know must move past a rogue thought and into a rhythm of thoughts that desire to know and be known.

Prayer has an intriguing dynamic of divine initiation that leads to human response. God is prompting or drawing us into a relationship. The thought to pray has never come from your desire for God but rather his desire for you. This rhythm is important to keep in mind. Regardless of how noble one's attempts may be, prayer does not begin and end with the individual. Prayer is our signal that we have relinquished our control and that God has dominion. In prayer, the divine image begins to re-form our identity, and we become both self-aware and aware that we are connected to God. It is simple; all of life is prayer—our coming and going, the big moments and the small ones that we forget about are prayers being offered to God.

Richard Foster, a brilliantly insightful writer in the area of the spiritual life, offers this idea of simple prayer to help begin our movement toward God: "In Simple Prayer we bring ourselves before a loving father, and we open our hearts and make our requests. We do not try to sort things out, the good from the bad."

There is an honesty that is required for this stage of prayer; we have to be honest about our desires. Prayer is an opportunity to be unfiltered, open, and assured that God accepts and approves of us as we are yet will not allow us to remain in our current condition.

Prayer is a formative process; it changes the one praying and it moves the heart of God, as seen throughout the Scriptures. Simple prayer is a movement toward God and away from the distractions that keep us at a distance from God. Simple prayer focuses our attention on God and reminds us that our heart—not our vocabulary—is what God hears when we pray.

Simple prayer is not about making prayer easier or reducing the amount of our lives devoted to prayer, it is about making it more accessible and more precise. I love the way *The Message* translation frames Jesus' words regarding prayer:

> Here's what I want you to do: Find a quiet, secluded place so you won't be tempted to role-play before God. Just be there as simply and honestly as you can manage. The focus will shift from you to God, and you will begin to sense his grace.
>
> The world is full of so-called prayer warriors who are prayer-ignorant. They're full of formulas and programs and advice, peddling techniques for getting what you want from God. Don't fall for that nonsense. This is your Father you are dealing with, and he knows better than you what you need. With a God like this loving you, you can pray very simply. (Matthew 6:6-8 *The Message*)

The following chapters are designed to introduce you to simple prayers that will deepen your faith, further your relationships, and lift you out of seasons of despair. Simple prayers are for every season of life and every stage of faith. A simple prayer is any prayer that is focused on God and prayed with an open heart, which allows the Holy Spirit to move in between the words to transform our monological prayer into a dialogical dance with God.

Simple prayers have been part of our spiritual heritage dating back to the third and fourth centuries. Simple prayers have been pivotal in my own spiritual journey and have opened my eyes to the fact that simple prayers may be all around us. They are in the Scriptures we read, the conversations we engage in, and even in the songs of worship that we sing. Simply stated, a simple prayer can be any phrase that your heart embraces and raises to God. Instead of prayers being lodged in our minds, these prayers become the prayers of our hearts.

2

Simple Prayer of the Heart

Lord Jesus Christ, Son of God, have mercy on me, a sinner.

PRAYER OF THE DESERT FATHERS

I grew up in awe of the way people worshiped with such freedom and prayed with passion and fervor. I would watch and listen to them, but secretly the experience gave me anxiety. I was paralyzed when it came to prayer. I never felt like my words were enough or that they were the right words to pray.

Prayer was this activity that was inviting and daunting all at the same time. People around me seemed to have no problem at all praying. I knew people who could pray for what seemed like days without trouble, while I felt like minutes were hours. It was a struggle, and I felt like my word count mattered to God, that my prayers were accepted based on the length or the volume of my prayers. Of course people told me that God listened beyond my words to my heart, but those people had all of the right words too, so that seemed a bit suspect. I wanted to connect with God in a deeper way but wasn't finding anything that helped me do that. I was growing discouraged. I needed prayer to not be so complicated.

My college encounters with the writings of ancient Christians shifted everything for me. My spiritual experience had been limited to my local congregation, where there wasn't much emphasis or awareness of the broad spectrum of Christianity. Our denominational affiliation seemed of greater importance than the breadth of historical Christianity, but I knew there was more and wanted to discover it. And in the ancient I found my future. The desert fathers, the Christian mystics, and so many other spiritual writers became friends along the way for me. These new friends turned out to be exactly what I needed. They introduced me to the simple—but not simplistic—Jesus Prayer. This simple prayer, which is both biblical and historical, transformed my prayers and my understanding of prayer for the rest of my life. Twelve words served as an invitation to something deeper than what I thought possible from a non-spontaneous prayer. This ancient prayer taught me that simple prayers make a significant difference in every aspect of life.

Lord Jesus Christ, Son of God, have mercy on me, a sinner.

These words became the rhythm of my soul. They guided me through ordinary days and seasons when extraordinary grace was needed. When prayer seemed too difficult, this simple prayer was there. The Jesus Prayer is a prayer of confession, and the Spirit moves between the syllables. God is always attentive to a cry for mercy. In the midst of seasons filled with tension, it is comforting to know that the same Spirit that hovered over the void at creation brings order in the midst of our chaos. I was accustomed to long prayers, passionate worship, and a readiness for the Spirit to speak through the Scriptures as evidenced by what came streaming out of one's mouth. Yet this "normal method" of prayer seemed to miss the mark at times. It was the minimalistic (or simple) Jesus Prayer emerging from deep within my soul that provided stamina in me.

TAKE ME TO THE DESERT

To understand the power of this specific prayer, we need to take a journey to the Egyptian desert to discover its origin. This prayer is not Western, and the approach is not normal for our linear minds. An understanding of the people and their approach to prayer will be helpful for us to understand the power in simple prayers. Often we come to prayer with our minds engaged and our hearts alone in the corner of the room. Prayer is not merely a mental function, nor does it separate our hearts from our minds. Prayer at its core is us being fully known and then being invited to know fully.

The Jesus Prayer is an invocation of the name of Jesus, an appeal for mercy, a confession of our sinfulness. The discipline of continual prayer that is fostered through this prayer enables it to become more than words. The prayer in its most common form, "Lord Jesus Christ, Son of God, have mercy on me," can be dated to the fourteenth century, but elements of the prayer were in existence much earlier. The prayer has both historical and biblical origins. It is found in the Gospel stories about the tax collector and the Pharisee and about the blind man on the road to Jericho.

When Christianity became legalized under Constantine in the early fourth century, some Christians fled the comfort of

communal living for solitude in the desert. After the major per-
secutions had subsided, some believers began to perceive a laxity
in the Christian faith, and retreat to the desert became more
popular than before. During this time, in the deserts of Egypt
lived a collection of monks, later known as the desert fathers,
whose writings focused on cultivating a continual remembrance
of God by using repetitive short prayers.

In addition to the verbal formulation of the prayer, these
monks also left inscriptions on the walls of monastic cells—
prayers composed of short phrases, discovered later and dated to
the time of the desert fathers. Personal letters written by two of
the Fathers known as the Old Men of Gaza gave instructions to
their laity to invoke the use of repetitive prayers focusing on the
phrase "Jesus, help me." One of their disciples used the prayer
"Lord Jesus Christ, have mercy on me, a sinner," and this is where
the prayer in its most complete form first appears.

Experiencing the presence of God is the quintessential desire
for the monk, and a life of prayer facilitates this experience. In
monastic life, prayer is rooted in Scripture both in origin and in
practice. The prayers were often part of the monks' daily routine
and allowed them to keep their mind focused on God throughout
their day. These prayers occasionally took the form of memorized
portions of Scripture—often a psalm. Similarly, the Jesus Prayer
initially emerged at this point in history but was not yet explicitly
identified as the Jesus Prayer. The themes essential to the Jesus
Prayer, such as internal stillness, compunction, and fleeing of one's
obsessive thoughts, however, are common motifs found in the
theology of the desert fathers.

THE JESUS PRAYER AND
EASTERN ORTHODOXY

The Jesus Prayer is an important prayer in the Eastern Christian tradition. The *Philokalia*, a popular book in the Eastern Orthodox tradition, describes and instructs its readers on the practice of the prayer as a central piece of their spiritual life. It would be a mistake to underestimate the power of the Jesus Prayer due to its brevity; its spiritual potency resides in the potential transformation of the one who prays.

Intrigued by this prayer and the immediate connection I had with it, I started researching it and trying to figure out where it came from. Part of me was frustrated that I hadn't found this prayer earlier, so I kept studying, searching, and practicing this compact prayer that was leading me into broader spaces. A depth in this prayer existed beyond the border of its twelve words. It was like the small door at the end of the hallway that leads Charlie and the others into Wonka's candy-filled world; the tiny door led them into a magnificent experience of chocolate rivers and everlasting gobstoppers. The Jesus Prayer was moving me past my words into a space of being with God that I had always longed for. I was finding my prayer life invigorated by this small, centuries-old prayer. It had been prayed countless times, and yet each time I prayed the words they were coming alive in me. This simple prayer was making a difference in my life.

One of my most influential discoveries was a nineteenth-century anonymous text, *The Way of a Pilgrim*. This writing was largely responsible for introducing the Jesus Prayer to a broader demographic.

Follow the pilgrim. In *The Way of a Pilgrim*, the pilgrim embarks on both a spiritual and a physical quest. The story catalogues the interior and exterior journey of a young man who sets out on a quest for the keys to a life of unceasing prayer as mentioned by the apostle Paul (1 Thessalonians 5:17), which most Christ-followers have thought to be either metaphorical or completely unattainable. Paul's challenge for his audience was to allow their prayers to be perpetual and without end, and the pilgrim questions whether this is truly obtainable. A journey across the countryside leads him from town to town seeking out wise spiritual elders who can offer advice on this interior adventure.

This journey brings the pilgrim to a monk in a small countryside town, and he asks the monk whether unceasing prayer is possible. The aged monk responds that it indeed is possible and brings him back to his monastery a few miles away. As they walk, the monk explains that this unceasing prayer comes only through the quieting of the mind and, in turn, making it one with the heart. The young man desires to learn a way to practice this prayer.

The monk begins to serve the young man as his spiritual director. He gives him a copy of the *Philokalia* and has him focus on the passages regarding the Jesus Prayer, and so his journey with the Jesus Prayer begins. The monk prescribes a certain number of prayers to pray in a day. In the beginning this is difficult, but eventually the task of praying the prayer twelve thousand times a day is a joy. The young man finds that the prayer is no longer an assignment; instead, it becomes the very breath in his lungs and greets him at daybreak.

What this pilgrim discovered in the Jesus Prayer is the underpinning of Eastern Orthodox spirituality, a spirituality connected to the desert fathers and mothers. This practice provides a rich experience that forms and enables a sojourner's life to be lived in rhythm with the Spirit, though not to the exclusion of the mind. The practice of this prayer can transcend emotional experiences and result in an intimate union with God. This simple prayer is the beginning of a much fuller experience with God.

I found myself identifying with the pilgrim journeying through the countryside, looking for answers to this invitation to a life of communion with God. For years the words of Paul had been a terrifying challenge, but I began seeing them as an invitation to a life of unbroken prayer. This concept seems tiresome to our Western minds, which tend to view prayer as a cognitive exchange—prayer is a problem to solve rather than a conversation in which to take part. Most of us only listen in order to respond, but prayer is more than us unloading our words, it is about getting to a place where words are not necessary. I want to be clear: the practice of simple prayer doesn't reject words but rather acknowledges that words are not the deepest form of communication. We know this to be true in our deepest relationships. There are bonds that transcend our words. When I am relaxing with my wife on a Sunday afternoon, I am not concerned with what to say as much as I want to be with her. Our nearness is more than enough. Words can actually get in the way. If we are enjoying each other's presence and one of us begins to talk about household chores or bills that are near due, the moments feel ruined, the connection lost.

What if our words are ruining our prayers? What if we have been taking moments of nearness, moments of intimacy, and cluttering them with words? Simple prayer allows our words to be precise, enables us to move beyond them, and carries us closer to God.

Four phases of prayer. To further understand the Jesus Prayer, it is helpful to have a framework of prayer in the Eastern Orthodox tradition. According to a respected Orthodox father and expert in the tradition, there are four phases of prayer. The first is external prayer. This is a form of verbally addressing God, including petitions for favors to be granted. Second is standing before God. This is done in silence, negating all discursive activities. In both these cases, the focus is on the human and not on the Divine. Naturally these first two phases of prayer are the most common to us. We make our petitions known or we come to God in silent reverence.

The final two phases are focused on the inner life and prayer itself. The third phase, inner act, is based on the teaching of the desert father Saint Gregory of Sinai and highlights the core experience in the Jesus Prayer. He writes, "True inner prayer is to stop talking and to listen to the wordless voice of God within our heart; it is to cease doing things on our own and to enter into the action of God." Here, silence is not the absence of voice but the willingness to listen for the inarticulate voice of God.

The final phase is the manifestation of baptism—not to be confused with the sacramental act, but as the embodiment of the Divine. This is the state of grace that is brought "to the point of full spiritual perception and conscious awareness when we experience and feel the activity of the Spirit directly and immediately." This phase allows our lives to experience the Spirit in rich detail with new eyes and emotions. It is a deeper connection with the Spirit and is essential in the full practice of the Jesus Prayer. The Jesus Prayer is not a mantra or an incantation; it is an invocation of the divine name in our midst. Our brokenness is made whole in the mercy of Christ.

THEOLOGICAL AND PRACTICAL
IMPLICATIONS OF THE JESUS PRAYER

Interior focus that leads to action is the fruit of the spiritual life. Various words are used to refer to this type of prayer—for example, meditation and contemplation at times overlap. Although these words are used interchangeably, for clarity in this discussion these terms will be more narrowly defined.

One writer states, "Meditation is an activation of one's spirit by reading or otherwise, while contemplation is a spontaneous activity of that spirit." Meditation involves intellectual rigor and requires more effort and energy. In contrast, contemplation requires the mind to be still and silent. When our goal is meditation, we begin a search; we embark on an adventure to be conquered or achieved. Contemplation is a journey that begins within the individual and grows out of an inner stillness. Contemplation is not beyond the capacity of the typical Christian. The contemplative life is open for all those who desire to enter into it. This distinction is important as we move forward with the practice of the Jesus Prayer.

The prayer is birthed out of a contemplative posture and can only be realized within a life that is engulfed by the prayer. This contemplative life is the entry to a life of praying without ceasing. The inner dialogue of the mind that takes place in contemplation is the place from which the Jesus Prayer emerges, and it is available for everyone. Achieving unceasing prayer is possible not only for the monk living a monastic life but for the Christian who desires communion with God as he or she goes about normal activities.

Contemplation is not the result of mental exertion. On the contrary, it is the absence of mental activity. This prayer relates to the Spirit beyond the heart or mind. It is not concerned with offering verbal prayers to be heard but with remaining in a posture that allows God to speak to us in a way that transcends language. This is not a prayer that is the result of intellectual assent but of a surrendered mind and heart. By providing an opportunity for confession, the prayer serves as a means of coming into communion with the presence of Christ.

Receiving instruction at Jesus' feet. Thomas á Kempis's *The Imitation of Christ* offers guidance for the spiritual life. In the section on the interior life, á Kempis writes, "Let all your thoughts be with the Most High, and direct your humble prayers unceasingly to Christ."

Luke records a story of Jesus at the home of Mary and Martha (Luke 10). He is invited into the home and finds himself in the living room. At his feet is a woman. Martha makes the preparations in the kitchen, while Mary ignores the things that need to be done in exchange for the only necessary thing—choosing to be with Jesus. This is a great image for our view of the role of the Jesus Prayer. There are lists and things that need to be done, yet one thing remains that is necessary: we are called to live in a deep relationship with God that goes beyond toil and preparation. This is a tragic commentary on our culture. We are preparing for a visitation when we could be reclining at the feet of Jesus. The Jesus Prayer offers us the ability to merge the two worlds together. The decision of Mary is at the heart of the instruction from á Kempis to live with our thoughts unceasingly on Christ. Mary prioritized being with Christ over working at a distance. Her choice received criticism and vocalized frustration from her sister, but she remained near Jesus. The fruit of a prayerful life is that we remain in Christ.

The primary aim of the prayer is to awaken the heart to the presence of Christ and to be enlivened by his love. This prayer of the heart journeys from the lips to the intellect, eventually making its home in the heart.

Parsing the Jesus Prayer. When the prayer functions in both the intellect and the heart, "it becomes prayer of the whole person—no longer something that we think or say, but something that we are: for the ultimate purpose of the spiritual Way is not just a person who says prayers from time to time, but a person who is prayer all the time." When we survey the content of the prayer, we see first that the name of the Lord Jesus Christ is the centerpiece. The New Testament refers to the name of Jesus as the name above all names (Philippians 2:9-10), the name that saves (Acts 4:12), and the name that the followers of Jesus invoke when making a request of the Father (John 16:23-24). Second, the prayer is a petition for mercy. The Greek word for mercy is *eleos*, which is frequently translated "compassion." This request for mercy serves as a reminder that regardless of status we are all broken and in need of God's mercy. Third, the Jesus Prayer is not a prayer of the virtuous but of the sinner. In a culture that encourages us to be inebriated with our own self-image and to have a skewed view of ourselves, the Jesus Prayer properly frames our life in view of Christ and our sinfulness. The prayer does not allow Photoshop to remove the blemishes on our soul; the phrase is simple, "a sinner." The prayer is one of repentance and turning away from our brokenness and shame while looking upward to God with hope.

PRACTICING THE JESUS PRAYER

Spiritual writers and sojourners agree on the essentialness of prayer, yet the practice of prayer in churches is nebulous—dialogue without practical application. This discussion without form or discourse creates spiritual confusion. Most people hear discussion about prayer but receive little instruction or space to grow in their knowledge of prayer. The importance of prayer is not questioned, but where are the spaces to practice or be instructed in prayer? I remember hearing, "You just have to pray and you'll get it." I am not sure why something so vital to the Christian life is left up to happenstance.

Creating a prayer atmosphere. The *Philokalia* is filled with hundreds of pages of advice about practicing the Jesus Prayer. Among them are instructions from the fourteenth-century monks Callistus and Ignatius, who were said to have left behind "full and perfect knowledge of the Jesus Prayer." They recommend that a person must first be earnest, undistracted, and in a place of absolute silence—silence being the most important thing to guard and the most difficult for us to find in a modern world. The surrounding room should be dimly lit. It is important to sequester potential visual stimuli. This is not a prayer that is to be practiced while reflecting on an image or imagination of Christ's teachings, miracles, or even Christ himself. The eyes can be either open or shut so that concentration will be solely on the prayer.

After arranging the external atmosphere, one can begin to focus on the process of allowing the mind to descend into the heart. The practice of closing one's eyes and bowing one's head comes from the instruction of the monks to give priority to the heart over the head. The Fathers recommend focusing your gaze on your chest as your head is bowed. When the *Philokalia* uses the phrase "prayer of the heart," it does not mean a prayer of emotions as in Western context, but rather a prayer of the total person. This prayer takes place in the body but is in rhythm with the soul and spirit.

Working through the levels of prayer. As the prayer begins, "breathe in: 'Lord Jesus Christ, Son of God'; breathe out: 'have mercy on me, a sinner.'" With each repetition focus on the words and allow them to ascend from the heart and not merely from the lips.

An Orthodox writer comments regarding the levels of the Jesus Prayer that are achieved during the experience, "Normally three levels or degrees are distinguished in the statements of the Jesus Prayer. It starts as 'prayer of the lips,' oral prayer. Then it grows more inward, becoming 'prayer of the intellect,' mental prayer. Finally the intellect 'descends' into the heart and is united with it, and so the prayer becomes 'prayer of the heart' or, more exactly, 'prayer of the intellect in the heart.'" The prayer begins as a prayer of words, but ends as a prayer of loving attention or gaze of the soul upon God. The end of the prayer is not an emptying of oneself but the experience of being filled with the Divine.

The prayer has two distinguished methods: free and formal. The free method is the use of the prayer throughout the day in normal activities. This use bridges the gap between times in worship and other explicit times of prayer; the prayer can become habitual and continuous during the simplest of activities, providing a cadence by which to live. The formal method can be practiced in a group setting but is most often done alone. A prayer rope may be used to keep track of the number of prayers offered. These ropes were used by monks who were instructed to pray the prayer for a specific amount of time or an assigned number of prayers. The monks' attention would be so focused on the prayer that they would use the rope to keep track of their progress. The mind and heart could be fully focused on the prayer while their hands kept moving across the knots of the rope. Two scholars note, "The purpose of the Jesus Prayer is summed up in this one phrase: 'Create silence.'" The essential goal is not the number of times the prayer is offered but that the prayer becomes a flowing stream.

Another application of the Jesus Prayer can be as part of the Divine Office, which gathers the global church together for specific times of prayer and reflection. While there is a prescribed liturgy for the Divine Office, the addition of the Jesus Prayer into this time has proven to be refreshing for me. When I discovered the Divine Office and the Jesus Prayer as a college student, I sensed that a new vista in Christian spirituality had been opened to me. As I connected with this ancient practice, I was being introduced to the larger family of faith, and with that came an expanded understanding of Christian spirituality.

What we seek in the Jesus Prayer is not analysis but invocation, not reflection but encounter. The Jesus Prayer is christocentric in nature. It moves beyond mere rhythm incantation that induces relaxation or concentration; the prayer is a confession of faith.

Thomas Merton became intrigued by the Jesus Prayer and noted that the prayer is a "state of imageless gazing." He goes on to add, "To pray in the spirit and in truth is to be highly effective. Prayer has far reaching political consequences." Prayer is a powerful activity. It renovates one's heart and mind while also having the ability to restore relationships with the world. Prayer produces awareness, and that results in an engaging life. Simple prayer refocuses our hearts on the true essence of prayer: being fully present to God in our interior lives and not just with our words.

The Little Prince by Antoine de Saint-Exupéry provides a beautiful window into the meaning of the heart in spiritual traditions: "Only with the heart can one see rightly. What is essential is invisible to the eye." When looking into the practices of the Jesus Prayer—or any discipline for that matter—one must keep this thought in plain view. Often beauty and wonder are sterilized when we try to see everything with the natural eye. It is quite possible that one's vision may be without fault and yet still unable to see the movement of the Spirit. The "prayer of the heart" was mentioned previously, but it is important here to define the heart's role in the practice. The heart is where encounters with the Divine take place, but it is also the place where darkness can dwell. In the heart one can come face to face with the power of darkness and sin. Our passions—the things to which we devote time and energy—can spur us toward God but are also the very things that can lead away from God. This tension is not resolved but negotiated.

A soul's gaze on God. It is not enough simply to recite the prayer without the soul's gaze on God. Irénée Hausherr writes, "Calling on the name of Jesus does not mean simply pronouncing the name 'Jesus' in prayer or directing a prayer explicitly to Jesus. There are some who say His name but who do not pray in His name." The same idea is present in Jesus' teaching in Matthew 7:21. Jesus warns his disciples that there will be some who call out, "Lord, Lord," and provide their list of spiritual practices and endeavors, but Jesus will tell them to depart—spiritual practices are not equal to being part of the kingdom. It is possible to be in prayer but never be *present* in prayer. The Jesus Prayer allows us to move beyond simple language and meaningless phrases, to cry out to God with both attention and affection. The Christian who prays only at formal times of worship is not living a life of prayer.

Prayers must make the confession that Jesus is Lord, not merely use the name as a key to unlock the door. The declaration of the lordship of Christ is critical to a prayer that is surrendered to God. It is not enough to pray because of requirement or to simply use language as a tool. Prayer must proceed from the heart. The one who desires a deeper level of intimacy with God must maintain a constant dialogue with the Father. To experience a transcendence that allows entry into a mysterious union with God, we must maintain a connection throughout the day. The Jesus Prayer seeks to keep us connected to the Divine while we interact with our daily routines.

My experience with the simple prayer known as the Jesus Prayer has been transformative. My tradition celebrated spontaneous prayers that were filled with boisterous language and emotion. I love those types of prayers, but what I found in the Jesus Prayer diversified my prayer life. I was finding a new depth in my prayers the simpler they became. The more concise the language, the greater their impact. The Jesus Prayer was my first experience with the practice of praying simply, but the intimacy and nearness of the Spirit nudged me to consider that this model of praying short, meaningful prayers and providing space for communion with God was a spiritual practice I wanted to explore. The Jesus Prayer helped me notice other simple prayers all around me. I would listen to people praying and hear their simple prayers. When I read the Scriptures, I began to notice voices praying simply. All around me were simple prayers, and the next few chapters will offer a few of them to you. Let them guide you, challenge you, and introduce you to a vintage way of praying.

3

Simple Prayer of Faith

Say the word.

PRAYER OF A ROMAN CENTURION

Help me overcome my unbelief.

PRAYER OF A DESPERATE FATHER

I have always been intrigued by the way the priests in the Catholic Church hear the confessions of the congregants. I am not naive enough to believe that the priest has the ability to forgive their sins or that anyone really believes they do—Christ alone is our forgiver—but I do love the healing power that comes in being able to hear a simple reminder of grace and mercy. There are moments when the thought of being forgiven isn't enough, but to hear the words "Your sins are forgiven, now go and sin no more" is very powerful. It can set us free from the doubts that have captured us.

In that spirit, I would like to begin with a confession. My confession is not one of misguided love or of rage that bubbles below

the surface. I have not embezzled money or been involved in a
Ponzi scheme. My confession is much less sensational and unseen
to most. It is a confession that is sometimes tough to share in
Christian circles, especially for a leader of sorts.

My confession is that I doubt. I have questions and am un-
satisfied by quick intellectual responses that attempt to eliminate
any other questions from emerging. In spite of the number of
sermons I have heard or delivered, these questions remain. I
sometimes look up in the sky thinking about all I have learned of
faith, hope, and love, shrug my shoulders, and say, "Really?" Now,
to be clear, I don't doubt the existence of God or other big pillars
of faith, but I do have difficulty believing that it all applies to me.
When I hear words like *grace*, *mercy*, and *forgiveness*, they are wonderful truths—I just find it hard to believe they include me.

For me, doubt isn't a whirlpool of disbelief but a bewildering
barrage of questions that flood my mind. Maybe you can relate
to this spiritual peek-a-boo: with more questions than answers,
you stumble upon an answer and it only leads you to more questions. Just when you get a glimpse, it goes away.

MY PRAYER IS THAT
I WANT TO HAVE FAITH

Over the years I have seen Christians who find it in vogue to
doubt or to stir up doubts. In my opinion, nothing could be
further from what we need. As humans we don't struggle with the
ability to doubt or find it hard to be a cynic; that is our natural
disposition. A beautiful hymn of the church captures our condition all too well: "Prone to wander, Lord, I feel it, prone to leave
the God I love." We naturally doubt. What we need is to cultivate

our faith. We need our prayers to be filled with faith and our lives lifted by hope. Some will find that easy, and others will need to find faith in order to have faith. The good news is that a cloud of witnesses cheers us on toward a life marked by a deep trust in what is hidden behind nail-scarred hands.

This chapter will look at simple prayers of faith we can hold on to that will stir up our faith—but first, a word on faith.

The writer of Hebrews begins the eleventh chapter with these words: "Now faith is the assurance of things hoped for, the conviction of things not seen" (Hebrews 11:1). Faith is the asset that all of our spiritual heroes possess. Faith is the key that unlocks the door to our own spiritual journey. Before Hebrews dives too deeply into a history lesson on those who had a faith worth following, it sets the ground rules. Faith at its core invites us into a mystery. It begins with being secure in knowing but not seeing, with being certain of what is just beyond our view. The writer of Hebrews then reminds us that the beginning of pleasing God is displayed in our faith. Our relationship with God starts with the essential element found in all relationships: trust.

ESTABLISHING TRUST

Trust is my preferred definition for faith. Trust is not an emotion that can be demanded or controlled; it is established. Trust in my marriage is greater now than it was in the beginning because we have mileage together. Each day adds to the life experience we share. We have a collection of memories built with lighthearted laughter and heartbroken tears.

I have always thought we had a marriage that could go the distance, but you never really know that until you decide to trust.

Speculation is never the same as participation. I learned early in our marriage that I couldn't demand trust; I had to demonstrate myself to be trustworthy, and that takes time. Our spirituality has the same rhythm. We can know that faith is a crucial element, but the underlying question remains: Is God trustworthy? This question can be aggravated by stories of injustice and suffering in which it seems that God is absent or not trustworthy. People can recall seasons of disappointment and wonder why God didn't come through.

Jesus assured us that in this world we would experience trouble, but he urged us not to worry because he had overcome (John 16:33). The power of the gospel lies beyond our present experience. The goal of our life is not to have an easier life with more stuff—that is the American dream—but to be reminded that all things are being made new. Our broken lives and our broken world are being restored, redeemed, and renewed. The trouble we have is that our theology is formed on a desire for a painless experience—a well-meaning thought that simply isn't biblical. The Scriptures offer us a clear picture: life happens, painfully at times, and it happens to us all.

The story of Job is one of the earliest writings in the canon. I find it fascinating that one of the first messages God desired to send to us was that suffering, pain, and loss are part of the human experience. They aren't signs of our lack of faith or of unconfessed sin, as some may suggest. This is life and it happens to us all. However, the most important message in Job is that when we experience suffering, our God suffers with us. We are not trusting in a God who sits off in the distance, peering through a window as we endure life's hardest moments. Our God has been in the room next to us all along. Our Savior knew suffering not so that we can avoid difficulty but so we can have confidence that we are not alone and that our God knows the way through suffering. God is near to us not to extract the pain but to mend us in the midst of our injury. When our friends have no idea what's happening and are filled with hurtful counsel, God is near. When the future seems to have perished, God's presence surrounds us. When those closest to us advise us to let go of our hope, God adjusts our vision to see not only our footprints but the horizon.

Job has a faith that has always astounded me. Great tragedy besieges him on all sides, and his trust in God remains. Moments of humanity remind us that when we experience suffering, our emotions become turbulent, but that doesn't mean we have lost faith. Perhaps our faith is established in times of trial. Perhaps it is in the moments when conventional wisdom says it's time to run, hide, or quit that our faith is fortified. I want a faith that remains in the moments when everything else around seems to be converting to chaos. I want to trust even when it is uncomfortable or unwise. Simple prayers of faith can lead us to that place.

So is God trustworthy? The answer is a resounding *yes*. All of the books in all of the world could not hold the stories of how God has demonstrated that he is trustworthy, but I will give you one: the cross of Calvary. The cross serves as a steady reminder that God is familiar with pain and anguish and that death is not the final word.

JUST SAY THE WORD

The Scriptures are ripe with phrases and statements that could transform our lives if we would hold them closely and allow them to become prayers for us. I remember a professor in my undergrad years who would challenge us to find ourselves in the narrative of Scripture: "Find the place where your life and the story intersect." The rest of this chapter offers examples of simple prayers that emerged from the story and collided with my life. The biblical narrative provided language I could grab hold of and form into prayers.

Matthew tells the story of a centurion who had a faith worth following and provides us with a prayer worth praying.

> When Jesus had entered Capernaum, a centurion came to him, asking for help. "Lord," he said, "my servant lies at home paralyzed, suffering terribly."
>
> Jesus said to him, "Shall I come and heal him?"
>
> The centurion replied, "Lord, I do not deserve to have you come under my roof. But *just say the word*, and my servant will be healed. For I myself am a man under authority, with soldiers under me. I tell this one, 'Go,' and he goes; and that one, 'Come,' and he comes. I say to my servant, 'Do this,' and he does it."
>
> When Jesus heard this, he was amazed and said to those following him, "Truly I tell you, I have not found anyone in Israel with such great faith. I say to you that many will come from the east and the west, and will take their places at the feast with Abraham, Isaac and Jacob in the kingdom of heaven. But the subjects of the kingdom will be thrown outside, into the darkness, where there will be weeping and gnashing of teeth."
>
> Then Jesus said to the centurion, "Go! Let it be done just as you believed it would." And his servant was healed at that moment. (Matthew 8:5-13 NIV, emphasis mine)

The Greek word for centurion is *hekatontarchēs*, meaning leader of one hundred men. Centurions were considered the backbone of the military and were responsible for commanding in the field and camp. Like anyone in a role of leadership, a centurion would have understood the importance of delegation, chain of command, and order.

Jesus is walking and is met by a rugged Roman soldier. Without introduction or an exchange of pleasantries, this man makes his request: "Lord, help. My servant is paralyzed, and it's bad. The pain is severe."

Jesus often asks the obvious question. This is not done in sarcasm; rather, Jesus uses this moment of panic to solidify the man's faith. At times our moments of great need are actually opportunities for us to move from simply recognizing who Jesus is to relying completely on him.

Jesus asks him, "Do you want me to heal this servant of yours?"

The centurion greeted Jesus as Lord, which for a Roman solider was a remarkable moment in itself. In the first century, Caesar was referred to as lord. The rulers of the Roman Empire were seen as deity; the cry of the Roman Empire celebrated them as gods. "Caesar is Lord" was on their lips and inscribed on the money in their pockets. To address Jesus as Lord was a confession of Jesus' authority and divinity, but what Jesus wanted was not a mere confession but ultimate trust. It is not enough to confess Jesus as Lord; one must believe that he is able to do the very thing that we are asking.

In the midst of this exchange, the centurion begins to think his worth will determine the response of Jesus. "I am not worthy for you to come to my house." Did he forget to make his bed? Were there dirty dishes in the sink? Why did he let his insecurity get in the way? Why do we? Somewhere in these conflicting thoughts—his unworthiness versus his great need—he offers an incredibly simple prayer for us to take hold of.

> The centurion replied, "Lord, I do not deserve to have you come under my roof. But *just say the word*, and my servant will be healed. For I myself am a man under authority, with soldiers under me. I tell this one, 'Go,' and he goes; and that one, 'Come,' and he comes. I say to my servant, 'Do this,' and he does it." (Matthew 8:8-9 NIV, emphasis mine)

TRUSTING IN JESUS

Just say the word.

Go ahead and read that again, this time a little slower. Can you hear the certainty in that line? It is laced with a confidence that whatever Jesus can do is not based on the centurion's worthiness, ability, or position. This prayer is both a declaration and a request. We pray this prayer filled with faith, declaring that with only a word our world can be restored. This prayer is at the same time a request for God to intervene. Offering this prayer lifts our focus to heaven while also shifting our hearts. Prayer is not intended to be complicated; it is supposed to be transformative. Prayer transforms our situations, our environments, yet most often I have found that prayer transforms us. Even in the moments when our prayers don't find the resolution we desire, they can transform us. I have had heartbreaking moments when prayers weren't answered, and the transformation that took place in me was that my prayers were more about getting the kingdom of God into my heart and mind than getting my way here and now.

We are being transformed every time we pray. This simple prayer transforms our ability to trust. I need to focus on my trust in Jesus in moments when I am disappointed. I find in those moments I need a simple prayer like "just say the word." What if we prayed with that same simple trust? Imagine how our lives would change if the prayers we offered abandoned us to Jesus like this one does. At the heart of this prayer is trust that Jesus can do more with a word than we can with any amount of effort. Sometimes my mind overrides my heart when I pray. My words may describe a trust but my mind tries to engineer a resolution. This prayer guides me to more dependence on Jesus' ability and not on my own.

The centurion's prayer displayed a deep-seated belief in who Jesus was and what Jesus could do. The stories about Jesus had circulated across the land—the teachings, the miracles—and his following was growing. People took notice when Jesus arrived. Just prior to this encounter, Jesus touched a leper and made him well. He touched someone considered untouchable. The miracle for this leper wasn't just becoming well; there was something very powerful in Jesus touching him. For years he would have had been stared at, been discarded, and had to pronounce himself unclean when approaching others. It was likely years since his last human contact. So an actual touch was the last thing he was prepared to receive from Jesus. Jesus not only meets obvious needs, he also desires to bring healing just below the surface. This leper wasn't just healed; he was made whole.

I want faith to believe that when Jesus touches me, I am made clean, but I also want a faith that doesn't need a touch for the miracle to come. Don't you want that kind of faith? A faith that doesn't consult circumstances and in the face of insecurities knows Jesus simply needs to speak the word—that is enough to make lifeless situations whole. Praying the centurion's simple prayer helps us move beyond often overwhelming details of our situations and predicaments and shifts us into a place of deep trust.

Praying this simple prayer of faith the same way that I pray the Jesus Prayer has strengthened my faith. These declarations become an echo in my soul. "Just say the word" has reminded me of the kind of trust that I want to mark my life. These prayers, like other simple prayers, are not exhaustive, nor are they supposed to be exclusive. This particular prayer refocuses my gaze on Jesus when I am in need of peace. It has also been a meaningful prayer when trusting God for a miraculous touch.

My daughter Hailey has a weakened muscle in her eye, which causes the eye to get fatigued and drift off its focal point. Each morning she wears an eye patch to help strengthen the eye. If her eye doesn't respond to the eye patch therapy, gain strength, and become able to focus properly, she will need to have surgery. Just the thought of that brings tears to my eyes, and I can feel the wave of worry flood my mind. While sometimes it is fun to sit around questions of "what if"—what could be—and be filled with hope and wonder, that same question can allow the entrance of paralyzing fear and uncertainty. The simple prayer of the centurion has been my weapon of choice in these moments. When I am confronted by the uncertainty of "what if," I find my way back to this simple prayer, and just above the roar of fear I can hear it resonate: "Just say the word." As I pray this over and over and allow it to be imprinted on my mind, I can feel my faith begin to steady. "Just say the word" reminds me that all my life needs is a simple word from Jesus. *Say the word and my daughter's eye is healed. Say the word and my fear of the future subsides in the confidence that you are powerful enough to send the word even from a distance.*

But what if you aren't there yet? What if, like me, you still have doubts? There is a simple prayer of faith for you too.

I BELIEVE . . . WELL, MOSTLY I BELIEVE

There is a story in the Gospel of Mark about a boy possessed by a demonic spirit that caused deafness and muteness to torment him. It was so bad that it threw him to the ground and at times toward fire or water to kill him. His father looked for a cure, but not even Jesus' disciples were able to provide relief. This must have been overwhelmingly grueling for this father. To see his son tormented like this meant that not just the son was bound by this demonic spirit—the father was trapped too. No child suffers without their parent also feeling pain.

As a parent, I hate when my kids are sick. I feel helpless and frustrated at life the moment their fever elevates. I would give anything to remedy their illness or to take the condition from them. Despite loving the extra cuddle time that undoubtedly comes, I would rather be running and wrestling with them. The sick version of my kids isn't the best version of them. This father in Mark must have spent countless moments crying out for help and searching for a cure. Desperately wishing that this condition could be placed on him to free his son, he longed for his boy to come back, and now not even the followers of Jesus could help him.

When Jesus comes to town, he is greeted by a throng of people; commotion is stirring to a fever pitch. A collection of voices was rising—some of them voices of confrontation and others voices of defense. These voices circled each other like boxers in a ring. The teachers of the law loved the fact that Jesus' followers were powerless, and the disciples had to have been embarrassed and perplexed as to why they were incompetent in this scenario. This poor man had come to the followers of Jesus looking for answers, and they had provided none.

Jesus is welcomed with the emptiness of their faith. He calls for the boy and, as the boy is being thrown into a convulsion, Jesus engages the father to diagnose the need. An evil spirit had bound the boy, but it seems the father was locked down by a problem that is native to us all: partial faith. "But if you can do anything, have compassion on us and help us" (Mark 9:22).

Before we are too hard on this father, look at what he has been through. He tells Jesus that his son has been like this since childhood. He has seen this spirit not only rob his child of hearing his father's voice but steal his ability to speak as well. On top of that, it has tried to kill him repeatedly. Life has worn down the father's ability to believe fully. The stories of what Jesus has done for others are good, but what is better is a personal experience. One encounter with Jesus is greater than a thousand stories about him. This father held stories and the testimony of others closely as he approached the disciples. His faith is frail and worn out, but he is there. He may not fully believe, but he knows where to go. When life wounds us and our faith is partial at best, Jesus can still respond. It is the fullness of who Jesus is that brings wholeness, not the sum of our faith.

HELP ME OVERCOME MY UNBELIEF

The confession of the father was the simple prayer that grabbed Jesus' attention. Simple prayers help us get to the core of it all. This father believed Jesus could heal his son but wasn't sure he would. Even in the midst of his "if"—his uncertainty, his doubt, and his exhausted faith—he had a moment of honesty with Jesus.

"I do believe; help me overcome my unbelief" (Mark 9:24 NIV).

This is the prayer of the saints of old and those becoming saints in this moment. If we are honest with ourselves, we acknowledge that we have all been there—and if you haven't, give it time; you will be. There are moments when we will hide this prayer in our hearts: *I trust you, Jesus, but there are places where it is hard to trust.* Sometimes our memory gets in the way of our faith. We remember moments when our faith didn't seem to help, moments when we wanted to believe but couldn't. Our history encroaches on the story God is writing in the moment when he calls us to trust fully.

The beauty of Jesus is that he can make things whole even with our wounded faith. This simple prayer gets us back to a place of honest devotion and trust. It picks us up when we are weak and unsure whether we can continue. It takes our simple trust and brings us to a place where we can depend on the words of Jesus, even when we are unsure that we have enough faith to matter. To embrace this prayer is to trust Jesus with our full condition, not just the part that we think will please him. Jesus isn't taken aback by our unbelief or our doubts. He isn't frustrated when our prayers shrink to simple forms to capture our truest self. Our true self is what he was after all along.

PRACTICING THESE SIMPLE
PRAYERS OF FAITH

These prayers are not intended to be difficult or overwhelming. They are intended to be inviting and accessible, simple phrases that can be easily remembered and convey our clear thoughts and message. Often our prayers become collections of thoughts and phrases to hide who we really are and what we really need. Simple prayer is about removing the pomp and circumstance from prayer and embracing honest language that can become a rhythm of prayer in your life. Such phrases can be repeated and provide a cadence to live by, or they can be starting points for your prayers to launch into the deep.

Say the word. There are moments in my life when I need to remind myself that it only takes a word from God for everything to be made right. This simple prayer has made my at-times shaky faith sturdier. What in your life are you believing or trusting God for? What do you need God to put right? This is a prayer that leans in and trusts that a word from the Word is enough. Take a moment to pray this prayer. Each time you say this prayer, fix your confidence solely in Christ. Resist the temptation to trust your talent or your ability to make something happen. Place your confidence in the power of the one who spoke all things into being.

An important disclaimer, of course, is that simple prayers are not guarantees that what you pray will come to pass. Too easily we look at prayer as an endeavor to get what we want from God rather than allowing our prayers to cultivate aspects of the kingdom life within us. Our prayers should be offered with a faith that has eyes wide open. We are not wishing upon a star with our prayers; we are being transformed into faith-filled followers of

Jesus who trust fully in the power of Christ. In the moments when our prayers seem to return only disappointment to us, perhaps this is the very time we reengage this prayer as a reminder that God is still able to do more than we could ever imagine in our lives with only a word.

Help me overcome my unbelief. Too many times in my spiritual journey have I come to places where my once-robust faith has fallen on feeble knees. There are moments when the reality in which I find myself is waging war on my faith. Have you ever been there? Have you wanted to trust God but you felt the disbelief overtaking your faith? This is a simple prayer that is filled with honesty, and that is the first step toward a deep place with God. Where do you find it hardest to trust God? Identify that, hold it in your mind, and then breathe through that thought with this simple prayer.

4

Simple Prayer of Forgiveness

Forgive us our debts, as we also have forgiven our debtors.

PRAYER OF A DISCIPLE

Father, forgive them.

PRAYER OF A SAVIOR

Have you found that forgiveness is easier to discuss than it is to put into action? I love the idea of letting the pain of the past evaporate like the dew on a blade of a grass in the mid-morning sun—I just don't like to actually forgive. I would prefer to hold on to the offense. I want to see the wrong made right; I demand justice. When a person speeds past me on the highway, I am not hoping that they get away with it. No, I am praying there is a hidden police car just around the bend with an officer waiting to catch them and write them a ticket. The shameful reality is that I plead for mercy when it's me who sees a police car out of the corner of my eye as I speed by. My passion to receive grace should match my passion to see others receive grace. This is what it means to love your neighbor as yourself: to hope for their well-being with the same tenacity with which you hope for your own. Following Jesus means walking in the footsteps of one who forgave greatly and continues to forgive frequently.

Some simple prayers require the heavy lifting of truly understanding what we are saying. Simple prayers of forgiveness are those types of prayers. This chapter will talk honestly about forgiveness and then introduce a couple of prayers that remind us of the power and responsibility to forgive. These simple prayers are some of the hardest for me to pray because they go against our natural inclination. They are reminders that we are not natives of the kingdom of God, yet we are called to affirm our citizenship.

FORGIVENESS GIVEN = FORGIVENESS RECEIVED

Jesus teaches the disciples how to pray with a collection of simple prayers that helps them grasp the connection between the prayers offered heavenward and the way their lives are lived with one another. The prayers move from honoring the Father with awe and wonderment to daily provision for our lives and even the rhythm of forgiveness.

"Forgive us our debts, as we also have forgiven our debtors" (Matthew 6:12).

This is a simple enough prayer, but its implications are significant. Jesus teaches the disciples that forgiveness received is based on forgiveness given. Our interaction with one another determines the interaction of the Father with us. Forgiveness means that I am releasing you from the debt of your offense and am no longer going to demand that you pay for your wrongs. The challenge comes when we view our need for forgiveness as less than someone else's need. It is easy to scroll through my Twitter feed and read snapshots of stories outlining the terrible atrocities that happen daily and whisper in my mind, *those people need forgiveness*, but forget my need for the same simply because my life is less publicized. Thanks be to God for a grace that is better than my behavior and forgiveness that overshadows my faults.

Often I lived trapped by the arrogance of my own piety. When I thought that forgiveness was a transaction that involved only Jesus and me, I had not fully understood the rhythm of forgiveness that Jesus taught. Giving forgiveness to another ensures that I can also receive forgiveness. The beautiful reality of forgiveness is that when I forgive, I am freed too. The tragedy is that when I choose not to forgive, I am held hostage. I move from being a victim to being a prisoner.

Think about it: we have all been wronged in situations where the offense was greater to us than it was to the offenders. We hold it close to our hearts, and the frustration turns to anger and then the anger grows into disdain. All the while the offenders have no idea their actions afflicted us with so much pain. We were the party being punished by unforgiveness; our refusal to forgive magnifies the initial pain. When I stop demanding it all be made right, then God can make all things new. I am not saying that we ignore the wrongs and the hurts that have wounded us. It is quite the opposite: stare each one in the face, become familiar with them, and then, in our woundedness, allow the presence of Christ to make us whole. Henri Nouwen captures this beautifully:

The man who articulates the movements of his inner life, who can give names to his varied experiences, need no longer be a victim of himself, but is able slowly and consistently to remove the obstacles that prevent the spirit from entering. He is able to create space for Him whose heart is greater than his, whose eyes see more than his, and whose hands can heal more than his.

The power experienced in forgiveness is greater than we realize. I have lived most of my life without any knowledge of my biological father. It wasn't until I was in my final year of college that the effect of this abandonment began to surface. I was completely blindsided by this. When unaware of something, you live with a blissful ignorance. When this woundedness was no longer hidden in the shadows of my soul, I had to deal with it. It was messy and required patience with myself. It was like untangling the extension cord in your garage—always a long process. It was a long journey to arrive at a place where I could forgive my father for disappearing. My tools for recovery were a Moleskine journal, conversations with mentors, the Scriptures, and this simple prayer of forgiveness.

Each time I prayed the words "forgive us our debts, as we also have forgiven our debtors," I became more and more aware of my humanity and my need for grace and mercy. I could not move forward in my life while carrying around unforgiveness in my heart. Bitterness doesn't lose its potency to destroy our lives just because it is justified. It was clear in the teachings of Jesus that my receiving forgiveness had everything to do with the way that I forgave others. This simple prayer helped usher in a new dimension of forgiveness in my own heart.

FORGIVENESS FOR DAYS

Jesus tells a parable in Matthew 18 about the kingdom of God and the role that forgiveness plays in it. The world as we know it exchanges money for power and exchanges influence for position. We have grown accustomed to seeing people climb over each other to reach their desired altitude of success, laying waste to ethics and friendships along the way. These are not modern problems native to our culture. They are human issues that have been around since the Garden of Eden, and they were around in the first century as well. Matthew, a recovering tax collector, intimately knew the beauty of forgiveness. When Jesus called Matthew to follow him, Matthew left his old life of greed and swindling his countrymen on behalf of the Roman Empire. It must have made for some tense moments as the disciples walked along the Galilean countryside with Matthew—the despised sellout who chose collecting money for Caesar over loyalty to his community. Matthew is the only Gospel writer who includes this parable, and that seems quite fitting.

The parable begins with Peter asking a question of Jesus: "How many times do I have to forgive my brother? Seven times?" (Matthew 18:21, my paraphrase). I love Peter and his questions; they are incredibly honest and at times terribly out of place. They sound like either a brilliant, symphonic melody or a missed note played loudly in the middle of a song. He frames his question with subtle hints of personal piety. Is seven times enough? Peter knows that Jesus, a rabbi, was well aware that forgiving the same trespass three times was sufficient. Jesus responds with an important clue on the temperament of the kingdom. He says to Peter, "No, try seventy times seven." Our veiled attempt to be righteous is seen in this exchange: when we think we have gone above and beyond, we are still not even close. Our ways are indeed lower than God's.

Jesus then leads into the meat of the parable about a master who desired to settle his accounts with his servants (Matthew 18:23-35). He tells of a servant who owed a large sum of money to his master and was unable to repay it. The master decided to auction off the servant and his family as slaves. The man cried out to the master, "Have patience, give me a chance and I will pay you back!" The master responded to this desperate cry with great mercy—he forgave the large debt.

The same man, having just experienced incredible mercy, then began looking for someone who owed him a very small debt. Once he found him he grabbed him by the throat and demanded to be paid in full. Then he heard the very words he had cried out to his master: "Have patience, give me a chance and I will pay you back!" Only this time he had the man thrown in jail, not to be released until he repaid his debt in full. The same cry of desperation met no mercy.

News of this got back to the master, and he was livid. "After all the debt I forgave you, you couldn't do the same for someone who owed you so little?" He immediately had the man thrown in jail.

Jesus looks at his disciples and says, "The heavenly Father will do the same to you if you do not forgive."

The currency of the kingdom is grace and mercy. The master in the parable forgives not because of the request of the indebted; he does so out of the goodness of his heart. Just as the master is filled with mercy, what fills our hearts will inevitably overflow into the other areas of our lives. What spills out of our hearts will tell on us. If our hearts are filled with greed and anger, even in the midst of mercy we will have none. It is not enough for us to experience forgiveness and then live our lives without any. That is not kingdom living. Kingdom living is when we understand forgiveness cognitively, embrace grace emotionally, and demonstrate mercy practically. The best beliefs are acted out. Jesus stresses to his disciples that the kingdom does not operate in revenge but in redemption. When we are looking for reasons not to forgive someone, we are not living with redemptive hearts—we are looking for revenge. Forgiveness and revenge cannot coexist.

I am convinced that our prayers matter. As much as they matter in heaven, they matter in our hearts. Prayers have the ability to change the course of my thoughts and inevitably my actions. Simple prayers keep the self-serving rambling out of the way and help start me on a better path. Prayers can help establish a rhythm or cadence to our lives. They help form us into whole-life followers of Jesus.

Jesus underwent the humiliation and embarrassment of a trial and subsequent flogging. His body was beaten and weakened. His followers, who had shared incredible ministry moments by his side, had either denied they ever knew him, gone into hiding, or exchanged their friend for a fistful of coins. Shockingly, disarmingly, and yet beautifully, this rejected, injured Jesus is the man Christians choose to follow.

To be a disciple is to be a student or a follower of someone. At the heart of this concept is the hope not only to gain knowledge but also to be able to extend our instructor's work in the spirit of the instructor. Paul captures this wonderfully in his letter to the church at Philippi. He writes, "that I may know him and the power of his resurrection, and may share his sufferings, becoming like him in his death, that by any means possible I may attain the resurrection from the dead" (Philippians 3:10-11).

Discipleship fosters intimacy and produces a desire to become one. Paul wanted to share in Christ's sufferings to thereby attain the resurrection, or to experience all things being made new. To follow is not to end up in the same place but to go along in the same manner. The challenge for us is to follow Jesus in his life and then embrace his death. The way of new life must come through death. Many times the new life arrives in the face of pain. The beautiful message of the Gospels is that new life emerges from a grave. Victory comes through what seemed like an incredible defeat. Our peace is often found after the pain. Before we can experience the new life of an empty tomb, we first must go through the cross.

THE SOUND OF FORGIVENESS

We can't miss this point: Jesus is forgiving the people who are killing him, at the very moment they are killing him. He cries out to his Father, "They don't know what they're doing." What didn't they know? These men were skilled killers and they were doing their job. They knew how to kill people. They had done this before and, according to history lessons, did it frequently. What they didn't know was who they were killing. On the surface, Jesus was a problem to erase. He and his tribe were a disruption and insurrection among law-abiding people. What the killers didn't know was that Jesus had come to make things new, and for that to happen something (or in this case someone) had to die. They had an idea but no real clue.

Jesus is hanging on a cross between two criminals and offers this cry of forgiveness. This setting demonstrates that forgiveness can come in the most unlikely of places and for the most unlikely of people. I can only imagine how those words echoed in the hearts of those who heard them. Regardless of what they believed about Jesus previously, this act of forgiveness transcended it all.

"Father, forgive them, for they know not what they do" (Luke 23:34).

What an incredibly powerful prayer to be offered on a cross! And it has the potential to be equally powerful in our own lives if we allow this prayer to reside in our minds and hearts. It is much easier to recite this than to pray it from our hearts. Simple prayers of forgiveness provide a reference point for us to use on the journey to forgiveness.

In July 2015, an act of terror occurred in the town of Charleston, South Carolina, at Emanuel African Methodist Episcopal Church; it claimed the lives of nine people during a midweek gathering. It is hard to comprehend such a violent demonstration of evil in a place that is supposed to be a place of refuge. The shooter was a white male, and the victims were all African Americans. They were not killed for being Christians; they were killed for being black. This was not a faith issue; this was an issue of racism and hatred. What troubles me about this tragedy is that it is not a story from the civil rights movement of the sixties—this is the twenty-first century. This and many other events that have been covered on the news serve as a reminder of the racial tension and deep seeds of hatred beneath our soil. I am concerned to contemplate what will happen when those seeds produce a harvest. Something must change.

As loud as the shots fired rang in that church (and in my own mind), the voices of the family members were even louder. Forgiveness has a sound.

When the loved ones of the victims were given the opportunity in open court to speak to the judge, in the presence of the person responsible for the deaths of their family members, their words resounded with a force greater than the impact of the bullets. They sounded like forgiveness; they sounded like Jesus. Each one of the survivors took the microphone and, without diminishing their pain, offered forgiveness in the midst of pain. Many of us don't forgive because we believe that we must be pain free to move beyond the wounds. Forgiveness isn't the aftereffect of healing; many times it is the prequel.

Shalom is a Hebrew word for peace and wholeness. We consider healing in overly specific terms in our Greek-oriented, Western minds. We think, *If my foot hurts, then my foot needs to be healed.* But what if the way that I walk is causing my foot to hurt? What if the way that I walk is due to the way my hips rotate while I walk? What if that is connected to a genetic defect in my back that creates the awkward gait? You see, healing my foot wouldn't take that all away. More than a healed foot, I need to be made whole. I need shalom in my body.

The prophet Jeremiah told the people headed to exile to pray for the shalom of the city they were in (Jeremiah 29:7). Essentially, pray for the wholeness or prosperity of the people who pillaged your land and dragged you away from your home. Those types of verses don't sit well with me. They serve as a clear reminder that the kingdom of God is much different than the kingdom I construct in my own mind. Our wholeness is experienced when we no longer allow the offense or offender to hold us hostage. We have all been wronged. We have all experienced hurt. We have all witnessed and felt the sting of hell on earth, and for many that hell is a daily occurrence. Forgiveness isn't saying it never happened, it is saying that you will no longer be a victim.

Forgiveness takes courage. Forgiveness has vision of a future where the present pain is a memory and no longer the focal point of our life. Forgiveness reframes what we have experienced and allows God to make us new. Just because we forgive, it doesn't mean that the wrong or the pain will certainly be made right, but I am so thankful that everything can be made new.

When Jesus forgave, he was on the cross. But his actions foreshadowed the empty tomb overcoming death. "Forgive them, for they know not what they do." Instead of wondering how we can beat evil, maybe what we need to do is look evil in the face and let it know that the greatest weapon we have is love. When the weight of forgiveness seems more than we can bear, remember, Jesus was fully human when he offered that prayer.

NOT HUMANITY 2.0

It is easy for us to look at Jesus like the physically gifted athlete in high school that happened to be one year older than his classmates. He seems just like everyone else, except he is better. But Jesus was not a better version of you and me. He was not humanity 2.0. Jesus lived a life empowered by the Spirit and followed the will of the Father—just like us. When Jesus was working miracles or teaching about the kingdom of God, he did these things as fully human, but his humanity did not reduce his divinity. Jesus laid down his divine attributes when becoming human in order to be the sacrifice needed for our forgiveness. If Jesus did the things Jesus did and was not human, then Jesus simply can't be followed. We can't be a disciple of a deity—that is impossible. However, if Jesus lived empowered by the Spirit and accomplished the will of the Father by way of that Spirit-empowered life, you and I have the ability to do the same. The voices of the South Carolina families echo this Spirit-empowered life that can offer forgiveness, even in the face of death.

Jesus rescues and reframes our present realities and delivers us from the pain of our present situations. His grace and mercy fill our lives, binding up the wounds of the broken, setting people free, declaring freedom for the captives, and interceding for those committing the wrong. We cannot bring healing if we are clutching on to unforgiveness.

Sometimes our situation is so filled with anguish that the only prayer we can muster is a simple one. Yet these simple prayers of forgiveness don't need many words because the only words that matter are the ones that unlock the chains holding us hostage. Each of these prayers has that potential.

PRACTICING SIMPLE PRAYERS OF FORGIVENESS

These prayers help us remain focused on living in a posture of forgiveness, ready to receive and give. We all need to practice giving and receiving forgiveness. "You are forgiven" can be hard words to receive and even harder words to offer. We know that our spiritual life is deeply connected to living a life of forgiveness, but I have yet to meet a person who has not struggled with either or both sides of the forgiveness coin. As followers of Jesus we are asked to not keep records of wrongs but to distribute forgiveness with an exceeding measure. These prayers are to be prayed slowly. Allow the words to find even deeper meaning in the memories they stir up. A great need for forgiveness is met with an even greater grace.

Forgive us our debts, as we also have forgiven our debtors. As you prepare to pray this prayer, allow your mind to be fully aware of your own faults and brokenness. Take notice of all the places in your life where you need forgiveness. Be mindful of the moments in life when forgiveness is needed most. Now as you consider your great need for forgiveness, let your mind turn its attention on the Lord. Don't rush past this. Feel the weight of your sin.

Begin to pray this simple prayer. Pray it slowly, considering each word and offering it to God. Allow your request of forgiveness to come from the place of deep awareness of your need for it. Repeat this prayer until you feel it settle into your soul. Let this become a prayer of your heart.

Now, just as the waves break against the shore, allow the tides of grace and mercy to cover your brokenness. Your great need of forgiveness has been satisfied. Receive this forgiveness. Allow it to release the burden of not forgiving from your heart. As you receive this forgiveness, may grace and peace renew your heart and mind. As you pray this prayer, also listen to the voice of the Spirit echoing in your soul: *you are forgiven*. Not partially, but fully.

Father, forgive them. Now allow your mind to consider the people in your life who need your forgiveness. Who are the people who have been reckless with their words and have caused damage to your heart? Who are the people who have let you down and have not been aware of how much their actions wounded you?

We are all aware that some wounds are not easily mended or forgiven, but the grace to receive forgiveness is also the grace to forgive. When we pray this prayer, we are drawing from that grace in order to move through these wounds.

Begin to pray this simple prayer. Pray it slowly.

When you ask the Father to forgive them, you are deciding to hold their fault against them no longer, which is what was holding you down all along. Forgiving others has a way of freeing us as well. This simple prayer leads us out of the despair of bitterness and introduces us to a rhythm of joy.

These simple prayers are prayers for every season of your journey. They are not easy to pray, and they are not intended to lessen the labor of forgiveness; they only serve our spirituality the way that rhythmic breathing serves a mother in giving birth. It aids the process, but the pain of delivery remains. We will always need to give and receive forgiveness. Having prayers that keep us focused on forgiveness is essential in living a life of freedom.

5

Simple Prayer of Unity

Become perfectly one.

PRAYER OF A CONCERNED FRIEND

Although I was born in the eighties, the nineties are the decade that influenced me most. In that decade I became a teenager and discovered my own way. The eighties offered me *Family Ties* and New Kids on the Block, but the nineties gave me *Family Matters* and Pearl Jam. There were some incredible moments and memories that the final decade of the twentieth century provided, but in one moment something I saw on the news shifted everything for me. I was eleven years old when I saw the beating of Rodney King playing on the news. I vividly remember watching with utter disbelief at the police taking turns beating him. I couldn't understand the excessive force and seeming disregard for him as a human. I watched a man be beaten worse than I had ever seen in my young life. One year later I was dumbfounded at the acquittal of the officers involved in the beatings. How could this be? I had heard that justice was blind, but how could it also be deaf and dumb? I was twelve when the city of Los Angeles went up in flames. The anger and the rage boiled over into destruction. Sometimes the lament of a community is heard in weeping, and other times it is seen in the gnashing of teeth.

We needed to pray for unity then, and we need to pray for it now.

It has been more than twenty-five years since that terrible night, and now I don't just see black men beaten at the hands of police. I am now seeing them gunned down with their hands up. My eyes have seen enough and my heart is heavy. I am overwhelmed by the images and grieved at the loss of life and brokenness in our country. Our first response at the loss of any life should be to mourn. It is a sad day when death visits anyone's door, and the church should be with people in their darkest hour. I am caught in this moment of pain and sorrow, and although my life may be insulated from these atrocities happening to me, it is not okay that these are happening to anyone. Dr. King said it powerfully: "Injustice anywhere is a threat to justice everywhere." I believe this is the bedrock of unity.

Jordan is an African American male in his early twenties. He recently joined our staff as a graduate assistant. He came into the office one morning and showed me a text message that his mother sent to him after a man was shot and killed in Oklahoma by a police officer. The text was begging him to be safe and, if he ever got pulled over by the police, to please be careful and not end up a victim. There was a level of terror and concern in her tone that I will never forget. I was visiting Copenhagen in 2015 when a terrorist attack took place the same day of my arrival. The text messages I received from my family didn't have the same fear and concern that this mother's message did for her son. As citizens of the kingdom we must understand that the King demands more from us than this. The worst moments of humanity are moments for the church to shine brightest. When despair looms like a dark cloud covering, hope becomes a beacon of light. God used words to create light; we are called to use prayer to illuminate areas of darkness.

PROPHETIC PRAYERS

I have always admired that Dr. Martin Luther King Jr. was a pastor. Before he was a political voice, he was a prophetic voice. The prophetic voice that we as believers are to embody must be raised in solidarity with the oppressed and downtrodden. The prophetic voice always provides a critique of anything that is anti-kingdom. Walter Brueggemann offers this thought regarding the need for a prophetic imagination: "Prophetic ministry seeks to penetrate the numbness in order to face the body of death in which we are caught." There is a numbness setting in to the church. I think this numbness arises when people truly do not know where to begin. People are silent when their voice needs to be heard, and people are wasting their breath within the white noise of social media. My friend Ray offered this thought regarding the flood of social media opinions: "Has social media produced any lasting change?" That is a question that we will have to continue to ask more and more as we are overstimulated by social media.

Our voices must be lifted to God in prophetic prayer, however, before we have any hope of a prophetic effect. God promises that if we humble ourselves and turn from our wicked ways, then our prayers will be heard and our land will be healed

(2 Chronicles 7:14). Our greatest forms of action are the prayers we pray. Healing comes when we have a change of heart and begin to take a step forward. To step toward something, we must understand that we are walking away from something. Praying this simple prayer requires the desire to walk toward unity. That first step is always filled with humility.

Unity of the believers. Jesus prayed for unity among the believers being left behind in the world, and if unity was a prayer worthy enough for Jesus to pray, it must be a prayer worth our time. The simple prayer of unity is needed now as much as it has ever been.

The church was in the forefront of social change in the civil rights movement, and now the church must move once again to the forefront and begin to bind up the broken. The ministry of reconciliation is at the foundation of the work of the kingdom, and we must take on that mantle. If we pray for unity, we must be willing to establish it with the work of our lives. Simple prayers are the prequel to powerful lives.

Jesus' prayer for us. I have always liked John's Gospel. He takes a different angle on the story than the other Gospel writers. The closeness of Jesus' friendship with John afforded him a more intimate look at Jesus, so his Gospel has elements not recorded in the others. It was as if John could see moments of beauty that the others missed. John brilliantly records the teaching and explanation that follow the Last Supper. Jesus looks toward heaven and begins to talk to the Father. This prayer is filled with care and compassion. It was a prayer for them—and for us, "those who will believe in me through their word." That prayer has a common thread throughout: unity.

"I do not ask for these only, but also for those who will believe in me through their word, that they may all be one, just as you, Father, are in me, and I in you, that they also may be in us, so that the world may believe that you have sent me" (John 17:20-21). Jesus' request was for us to be together as he and the Father were one. This desire has inspired a simple prayer to emerge in my heart: *Father, make us one.*

Now more than ever we need to unify. For all the advances in our society, we are not progressing in our nation in this area. We are fractured and in need of healing. We must take note that segments of our society do not feel heard or valued and, even worse, do not feel safe. To believe that all lives matter equally is to agree that we are created equal and in the image of God, but to ignore the discrepancies in our nation on this topic is to place a blindfold on our eyes so we can avoid the clear chasms of inequality. This season has reminded me of a simple prayer that I feel we need to embrace. It must be both our compass and our conviction.

THE KINGDOM HAS COME

As followers of Jesus we are commissioned to minister in the same spirit, empowered by the Spirit. Luke's Gospel provides us with incredible insight into prayer, but it also has much to say to us regarding what the kingdom of God is like. The kingdom of God is not designated to a political system, nor does it submit to national pride. Too often our personal preferences are held up as kingdom ideals, but they may in fact be at odds with the kingdom of God. There may be issues that are important for a nation to consider, but the people of God must keep in clear view that what is good for our nation may be opposed to the kingdom of God. And the kingdom doesn't debate its position.

Jesus clearly proclaims this truth upon returning to his local synagogue after his baptism and forty days in the desert. His message gives the people a clear picture of the work of the Messiah and what the kingdom of God is like:

> "The Spirit of the Lord is upon me,
>> because he has anointed me
>> to proclaim good news to the poor.
> He has sent me to proclaim liberty to the captives
>> and recovering of sight to the blind,
>> to set at liberty those who are oppressed,
> to proclaim the year of the Lord's favor."

> And he rolled up the scroll and gave it back to the attendant and sat down. And the eyes of all in the synagogue were fixed on him. And he began to say to them, "Today this Scripture has been fulfilled in your hearing." And all spoke well of him and marveled at the gracious words that were coming from his mouth. And they said, "Is not this Joseph's son?" (Luke 4:18-22)

After Jesus reads the passage from Isaiah, he informs his listeners that the passage has been fulfilled that day. Isaiah begins with the phrase, "The Spirit of the Lord GOD is upon me" (Isaiah 61:1). Given his previous experiences in the desert and at his baptism, Jesus does not necessarily give a simple reading but makes a statement. The power of the Spirit residing in the life of Jesus is the foundation of the ministry of Jesus. His ministry is not marked by effort, skill, or pedigree but by the power of the Spirit. He boldly uses messianic language, and the people respond favorably. One of their own was the Anointed One. All eyes were fixed on Jesus as the people intently awaited his next words.

The people's astonishment and praise end abruptly when Jesus begins his instruction. Jesus' language doesn't merely ask a question; his tone is filled with accusation. He makes the point that those who are hearing about and now seeing the Messiah have no idea what he and his kingdom are concerned with. Jesus confronts the hearts of the people in his hometown. It is easy to imagine the conversations Jesus heard growing up in Nazareth: everything will change when the Messiah comes. But the change that had been anticipated was self-centered. When Jesus unravels their understanding of the Messiah, the people move from astonishment to rage.

His teaching hits a boiling point when Jesus remarks that the only leper to be healed in the ministry of Elisha was Naaman, the Syrian (2 Kings 5:1-14; Luke 4:25-27). Naaman was a general in a foreign army; he was not one of them, not a Jew. This defining message from Jesus about the mission of the Messiah is inclusive, allowing the foreigner to become a member of the community. The very location of Naaman's healing is where Jesus was baptized before entering the synagogue to deliver this announcement.

The people move from awe to anger and they drive Jesus out of town to a cliff's edge to throw him to his death. Jesus' first message declaring that he is the Messiah nearly gets him killed. It is not the message that enrages them; it is the inclusive nature of the message. The people who were fans of Jesus want to kill him. Their expectations of the Messiah and his reign were based on their desire to become the powerful ones, the focal point of society. The kingdom has arrived and its message is inclusive; this is truly good news—unless you had been hoping for exclusivity.

As participants in the kingdom, we must ask, Where are the outcasts? Who are the broken? Who are the forgotten or marginalized? Once we identify them, then we must make room for them at the table. We must draw near to them. The incarnation demonstrates this, and the cross of Christ demands we become people of reconciliation.

Our simple prayers must align with the mission of the kingdom. Our prayers are opportunities to become congruent with the activity of God; otherwise they become vain attempts to forge our own way. It is a terrible thing to hope and pray for the Messiah to come and then try and kill him when he reveals that his kingdom looks a little different than expected. That's what Jesus' hometown did, and if we aren't careful, we can do the same.

MORE THAN A FEELING

Sometimes our prayers are simple and the desired outcome is intimacy, but this simple prayer is prophetic. Simple prayers remind us that we don't need many words when we have the right ones. For there to be unity we must move with compassion. This prayer is more than passion, it is action. The simple prayer—*make us one*—must be prayed with fervor to overcome areas of division and begin to see areas of brokenness.

When the writers of the New Testament use the word *compassion*, they are literally speaking of being moved internally, deep in your guts. Compassion takes guts. The desire to be unified requires them. Compassion requires a response; it motivates us to action. Jesus had compassion on the crowd because when he saw them "they were like sheep without a shepherd" (Mark 6:34). He was so moved, he responded. At times it was with a touch. Other times it was with a word of encouragement, but ultimately his compassion for humanity caused him to give his life for us.

Another example of compassion is found in the story of the good Samaritan (Luke 10:30-37). Only in Luke do we find this parable, which is fitting given the message represented in the story. Jesus contrasts the lack of compassion by a priest and a member of the tribe of Levi with the kingdom-like compassion that the Samaritan provides. These were roles that the hearers would not have seen coming. The outsider is the exemplar and the unifying agent in the community. Without compassion our words would never become actions. Compassion isn't just the awareness of a need but a willingness to meet that need. Compassion inconveniences self to attend to someone in need.

BIG SKY AND A BROKEN HEART

I remember standing on a street that ran directly through the heart of downtown Bozeman, Montana, after receiving a call that the child we were expecting in three short months had passed. Surrounded by the big sky of Montana, I was finding it hard to take a breath. I had just gotten off the phone with my wife, who was as broken as I have ever heard a person. I could almost feel her tears on my cheek as she filled me in on the details of the doctor appointment that revealed that our unborn child didn't make it to term. We were in the third trimester and filled with hope and anticipation for this little life to join our family. We were devastated.

The trip to Montana was a writing retreat, and my friend Jeremy and I were having a blast. We would write during the day and enjoy the beautiful view of the Pleasant Valley scenery all around us. The mountains were covered with snow and seemed to frame every picture.

But that night in Montana was dark, and even darker for me. I was bewildered and angry. I was hurting and didn't know how to make the pain subside.

Jeremy was the perfect companion to me that night. His wife has been recently diagnosed with Huntington's, a neuro-degenerative genetic disorder that affects muscle coordination and leads to mental decline. There are no known cures or re-coveries recorded. Jeremy and Tiffany had watched her mother succumb to this disease after a fifteen-year struggle. He has to deal with his wife slowly disappearing before his eyes while also knowing there is a significant chance one or more of his kids will suffer the same fate. He was familiar with the feelings of bewilderment and hurt that were like a raging flood in my mind. He was too familiar with the terrible things people would say in the spirit of meaning well. His companionship to me that night was a grace. I am not sure how I would have made it through that night without his friendship. I have looked back on that time and remembered him saying, "Wherever you want to go, whatever you want to do, I am with you. If you want to talk, we can. If not, that's fine. I am with you." His words were simple statements with a profound impact.

Our prayers can be like this: simple in structure, profound in impression. Prayer moves us beyond our words, and this simple prayer for unity must do the same. Unity begins with a humble heart that desires to listen more than to be heard. Do you try to make your voice heard before embracing the voices around you? It is hard to be unified if we always need to be right. Unity means we lay down our point of view for a vision of the kingdom.

PRACTICING THIS SIMPLE PRAYER OF UNITY

To be honest, this is not a prayer for the faint of heart. This prayer, like most prophetic work, requires resolve to remain when the results seem far off. The work of a prophet is neither convenient nor easy. This prayer takes a lot out of you but also puts more into you. This prayer comes directly from the heart of Jesus, and is a great need in our world today. We can look around our country and see that the church is not currently one. Our divisions are becoming more and more significant. This simple prayer is needed as much now as when Jesus prayed it.

Yet praying this prayer is only the first movement for those who long to see Christians unify on behalf of those who suffer. I love the story in Acts 12 of Peter in prison and the church praying in solidarity with him. They were unable to change the situation, but their prayers activated the angels who set Peter free. Our prayers are the action that matters most.

Jesus did not merely know the mission of the Messiah so he could recite it in a church service. He was propelled by it. His life was a demonstration of the calling to be the Messiah. We also have a calling: we too are called to participate in the kingdom of God. Jesus announced that the kingdom was different than expected. Do we read those words from Isaiah with the same conviction? Does the anointing of the Holy Spirit lead us into greater service and solidarity with the broken? Are we filled only with messages to preach and teach rather than lives to live out in prayer? This simple prayer is a constant reminder that in a nation where division or indifference rather than solidarity among those who confess Christ seems to be the norm, we commit to praying for unity. This is a simple prayer that must first be prayed and then be acted upon. Praying for unity is the prequel to establishing it.

6

Simple Prayer of Restoration

Have mercy.

PRAYER OF A BLIND MAN AND TAX COLLECTOR

He restores my soul.

PRAYER OF A SHEPHERD WHO BECAME KING

There is something beautiful about restoration. I have a friend who owns a store in downtown Lakeland, Florida. Her store, Simple Vintage, takes restoration to a new level by capitalizing on making old things new. *Upcycling* is a term that I have heard used in the shop. My friend and her team take vintage items and refresh them. My wife and I have been so captured by the charm and uniqueness of items from this store that we have purchased many of them for our home. Each one of them has past experiences, yet each one now sits in our home telling a new story. They have a new purpose. My favorite is the dresser in our bedroom. It is a classic French provincial dresser, a style typical for the French countryside in the 1600s. This type of décor displays basic lines and uses simplicity to demonstrate beauty. Our piece has been refinished with an antique white chalk paint that has been distressed just enough to allow the dresser's former finish to emerge.

There is something very spiritual about what takes place in that store. Each item has a story locked inside that needs to be restored. Restoration returns things to their original intent. There is a thin line between trash and treasure, and it takes a special person to see potential in the trash and bring that to life. Vision is not just an organizational phenomenon; vision is profoundly personal. Vision is transformative, and restoration requires vision. Someone must be able to look past the external and see that there is something more beneath the surface. Kim, the owner of Simple Vintage, has an incredible ability to see things lying on the side of the road and breathe new life into them.

The Gospels are filled with these moments—moments when the old is exchanged for the new, when purpose is restored.

Restoration begins with a simple cry for mercy. This cry is filled with an honest confession of surrender, an honest declaration of being unable to go any further. This is the spiritual equivalent of crying uncle. Restoration is the preferred future of the broken, but the journey begins with surrender. Striving and mercy can't occupy the same place at the same time. Mercy is truly experienced when we stop trying to achieve it and simply receive it.

Luke's approach to telling the good news of Jesus focuses on the theme of inclusion, which is foundational to the kingdom of God. When the surrounding political kingdom's powers build barriers to keep some in and others out, Jesus represents God's kingdom by announcing a simple message: the kingdom has arrived and everything is different. This message invites in those on the fringe, the outcasts. It invites them into places where they don't belong or where people wouldn't have expected to see them.

Luke's Gospel offers a few narratives for us to consider to better comprehend how prayer, mercy, and restoration are connected. Luke tells us more about prayer than any of the other Gospel writers. His message is simple: prayer is a central part of our everyday lives, and it isn't intended to be just a functional duty. Prayer is the core of our spirituality and should be intertwined into each moment of life. Every second of our lives is an opportunity to pray simple prayers. Those prayers lead us into moments of restoration. Jesus invites us in as we are and loves us enough not to let us stay that way. Luke uses two tax collectors and a blind man to teach us about a cry for mercy and the restoration that follows. The first tax collector is a fictional character in one of Jesus' parables, an unlikely hero.

TWO GUYS WALK INTO A TEMPLE . . .

Jesus tells a parable among a group of people that was known to be self-righteousness and not very friendly. The characters in Jesus' parable would have been familiar to his audience. These two characters would have evoked internal emotion for the hearers as Jesus began the parable. It would not have been typical for Pharisees to be portrayed as antagonists since their position was one of built-in respect within the community.

This parable begins in Luke 18:10 with two men going up to the temple to pray. Psalm 24:3-6 poses the question about who may ascend the hill of the Lord, and these requirements are given: "clean hands and a pure heart." The Pharisee is found lacking in at least one of these requirements. The villain in this story is the Pharisee with his pride-filled heart. While Pharisees were leading religious figures in the nation, Jesus criticizes them and befriends tax collectors, who were typically seen as revolting members of the community. When the audience heard the parable they would not have shared Jesus' point of view. Instead they would have had a positive image of the Pharisee and a negative image of the tax collector. The two men enter the temple with distinctively different postures, both externally and internally.

According to Luke, Jesus' inference in this parable emphasizes one quality in each man: one claims superior status for himself by comparing himself with and separating himself from others; the other makes no claim to status at all but rather acknowledges his position as a sinner who can take refuge only in the merciful embrace of God.

Rush hour in the temple. What is striking at the outset of this parable is the ease with which Jesus says that the tax collector went to the temple to pray. While it would be customary and even expected that a Jewish man would go to the temple for prayer, this man is a tax collector. It is not likely that he would want to be identified as such in a public way. That means that any hearer of the parable would never have heard of a tax collector going to the temple to pray. The effect is a rather shocking spectacle within the narrative.

The temple had rhythms throughout the day that included sacrifices, commerce, instruction, and both public and private prayer. This parable likely takes place during one of the public prayer services, known as the *Tamid* services, at either 9:00 a.m. or 3:00 p.m. Dennis Hamm maintains that during the Second Temple period it was not the annual atonement service that dominated the Jewish imagination; rather, it was the twice-daily, whole-offering *Tamid* service. When we read that two men went up to the temple to pray, we imagine two individuals "making a visit" to something like a church for a moment of private prayer. Yet this parable begins with a scene of a "great assembly of the people" gathered for prayer in the temple precincts at the time of the afternoon *Tamid*. This provides a clearer cultural understanding of the scene in which both men enter the temple to pray.

Standing, as the Pharisee does, is a normal and accepted posture for prayer, but the location of his standing may add to our understanding of the narrative. Hamm suggests, "We are not told directly, but a comparison with verse 13 may indicate that he stands as close as possible to the actual sanctuary, with its Holy Place and the Holy of Holies." In this locale he offers the prayer of thanks that he is not like the rest of humanity, which reveals the arrogance in his heart. The prayer is outwardly being offered to God, but he is actually talking about himself to himself. This prayer is for his ears as much as it is an offering to God. He is exalting himself and denigrating others, particularly the tax collector.

The Pharisee offers a prayer of congratulations and celebration about himself for all that he has done and the areas that he has refrained. A possible translation for Luke 18:11 could be, "The Pharisee stood up and prayed about himself." One could wonder, can he only feel good about himself if he has others to condemn by contrast? Humiliation of others ought not be the prescription to increase one's self-esteem. It is intriguing that the Pharisee did not use other devout men as a measuring rod; he viewed his piety in comparison to an outcast or a person who was despised in society. When piety is dependent on the perceived morality of those around us, it is much easier to view ourselves as holy. In his claiming not to be guilty of robbery, he is misappropriating his piety to be focused on what he has refrained from. He uses the tax collector, who would typically have been thought to be morally bankrupt, to highlight and boast in his self-righteous acts. But piety is not based on performance in relation to our peers; it is based on having a heart and life that are honoring to God. When self-promotion becomes the focal point of religion, the righteousness that we boast in is our own and we forfeit the justification offered by God alone.

Meanwhile, the tax collector enters the narrative "standing far off" and begins to pray (Luke 18:13). Both the manner and content of this prayer are set in contrast to the prayer offered by the Pharisee.

The tax collector stood "far off," meaning that he stood at a distance from one or more of three things: the Most Holy Place, the Pharisee, or others at prayer. In fact, if he was far off from any one of these, he would have been far from all three, standing in an outer courtyard of the temple as a sign of unworthiness before both God and others. Instead of assuming the usual posture for prayer—that is, standing with eyes and hands uplifted (see Psalm 123:1; John 11:41; 1 Timothy 2:8)—the tax collector would not raise his hands or eyes.

His posture is a sign of shame and guilt and is accentuated by the beating of his breast in anguish or contrition. The prayer of the tax collector is not one of thanksgiving; it is a cry for mercy. The tax collector beats his chest and says, "God, have mercy on me, a sinner" (Luke 18:13 NIV). This is a distinctly different prayer than the prayer of the Pharisee.

A simple prayer for mercy. The content of the tax collector's simple prayer, a cry for mercy, contrasts with the overbearing and long-winded prayer of the Pharisee. The cry for mercy is not the more common plea of *eleēson* ("mercy") as previously used in Luke's writing (Luke 16:24; 17:13; 18:38-39). This cry for mercy uses another Greek word that carries significant meaning given the location of the prayer—the temple. The word *hilasthēti* is the imperative of *hilaskomai* ("to show mercy"), a term also used in Hebrews 2:17, where it refers to Jesus making atonement as our merciful high priest. This is atonement language.

In this passage, *mercy* means "to make atonement or amends for," which is appropriate given the setting of the prayer. The request of the tax collector is to be made right, to be made clean. The prayer is offered in the temple, the place where atonement for sins is made. It would be expected at this point that there was no way that the tax collector, on the basis of prayer alone, could have been forgiven. The Old Testament provides a model that would have expected the tax collector to give up his profession and make full restitution with an additional one-fifth added (Leviticus 6:5; Numbers 5:7). Yet the text states that the tax collector went home "in the state of being justified" by God. This justification is instantaneous, and this parable reveals that the theme of justification, often attributed to Paul, finds its roots in the Gospels.

The mercy shown to the tax collector demonstrates the theme of inclusivity woven throughout Luke's Gospel. The tax collector is not left on the outside of the kingdom looking in; he is invited in. This different word for mercy signals that more than a physical kingdom is in mind—a spiritual kingdom is envisioned as well. There are continuing holistic effects of this gift. This mercy leads to full restoration. You will see this explicitly in the invitation to Zacchaeus, a chief tax collector, to share a meal with Jesus.

When in previous passages Luke refers to mercy that isn't connected to atonement, it applies to the sick being relieved of physical turmoil, as in the story of the rich man and Lazarus. The man with leprosy and the blind beggar on the road to Jericho are also examples of this cry for mercy being connected to rescue and relief from ailment. Here in Luke 18, *hilasthēti* makes a connection to the place of the prayer's offering—the temple. The plea for mercy is tied to the need to be justified, not merely rescued. This is not to diminish or exalt one term over the other, but rather to properly frame the concept. Both *hilasthēti* and *eleēson* are pleas for mercy; they are cries to be restored. The tax collector asked for much more than the healing of a disease or rescue from torture. He was aware of a relational fracture that needed mending. Justification deals with the restoration of a damaged relationship, not just a pardon for the offense.

The Pharisees sought to justify themselves in the sight of others, but their prayers fell upon deaf ears. The result is that the tax collector left justified and the Pharisee left the way he had entered the temple. The physical act of praying is not enough to bring about a restored relationship with God. God responds with mercy to a contrite heart.

We all know that what we say is only a portion of our communication. The nonverbal messages we send are as important if not more important than the words we use. Prayer is no different. Our hearts scream much louder than the words we offer. The Pharisee had all of the right words, but his heart told on him. Simple prayers are mindful of the space between the words we offer, in which our hearts are revealed. The space between the words holds the true meaning of what we are communicating. It focuses our attention and affection toward God and then allows room for the Divine to act.

The heart of the matter. Two contrasting emphases can be seen in this passage: moral achievement and begging for pardon. The Pharisee exalted himself above all other people, especially the tax collector. However, the posture of the tax collector was one of humility and contrition. "The audience of the story in Luke's Gospel is left with two options, they could see themselves in the story or could become angry with Jesus."

We can do the same. Simple prayers can keep us from becoming like the Pharisee. We can align our hearts with the tax collector, who knew he would be accepted and restored based only on the mercy of God, or we can be like the Pharisee, who let his pride get in the way of his prayers.

When Jesus uses a parable, he doesn't seem to care much about telling us an abstract truth. He tells stories not to inform or define but to introduce the ways and will of God into the homes, neighborhoods, and workplaces in which we spend our time. It is not enough for our prayers to sound holy; the heart that offers the prayer must be congruent with the heart of God.

SITTING, WAITING, WISHING

After Jesus does some teaching, he pulls the disciples aside and tells them that they are headed to Jerusalem. His purpose is to be fulfilled there. Just before Jesus and the disciples arrive in Jericho,

their travels are halted by the cry of a blind man named Bartimaeus seated on the side of the road (see the parallel in Mark 10:46
for the beggar's name). Those around him demand his silence,
"but he cried out all the more." His persistence no less than his
volume catches Jesus' attention. Bartimaeus's message is simple:
"Son of David, have mercy on me!" (Luke 18:39). His cry comes
from a deep place of need, a place in his heart that longs to experience life with all five senses. It isn't enough to feel the sun; he
wants to be able to see the sun dance across the waters. His
identity is wrapped up in his condition.

The crowd gathers and grows in number to catch a glimpse of
Jesus, the Son of David. While everyone else sees this as a part of
the journey to somewhere else, Bartimaeus sees this as a moment
of destiny. It is fascinating that the people who possess sight are
preparing for a parade, and yet the blind man can see more clearly
than them all. There is something significant in this simple, ordinary moment. As he hears Jesus approaching he begins to cry
out, "Son of David, have mercy on me."

The phrase "Son of David" is a messianic confession. Bartimaeus is appealing to Jesus as the answer to his broken condition.
He is asserting that this Jesus is the one, the Messiah they had
been waiting for. Bartimaeus knows that Jesus can restore his
sight. What he needs is for Jesus to have mercy.

Bartimaeus's voice reaches the ears of Jesus, and Jesus calls for
the man to be brought to him. What was it that captured the
attention of Jesus? I imagine there was ample noise and chatter
among the crowd, yet it couldn't drown out the blind man's plea. The
louder and louder he grew, the more the people tried to silence
him. It wasn't just his request that caught Jesus' ear; there was

something in the request that captured Jesus' attention. Bartimaeus wanted mercy.

Jesus asks the question of a lifetime: "What do you want me to do for you?" (Luke 18:41). Bartemaeus's cry for mercy is more than just a physical or spiritual request. It speaks to his deep desire to be made whole. This mercy would change everything for him, not just being able to see. His begging days would be no more. His position in society as an outcast would begin to fade away. When mercy is given, it has a way of changing more than just what we ask for.

This question—"What do you want me to do for you?"—was also posed to a group of the disciples who at the time were maneuvering for position in the kingdom (Mark 10:36). They were fighting about whose seats would be closest to Jesus. Their hearts' cry was for power. The difference between the disciples and Bartimaeus was the motivation of their hearts. One offered a humble cry for mercy, while those soaked in their own pride asked for positional blessings. The motivation for the beggar was purer than the disciples' goals. From time to time even those closest to Jesus lose sight of what really matters, and here a blind beggar has perfect vision. After receiving his sight, he finds his way into the band of disciples headed toward Jericho, and off in the distance they see what seems to be a man in a tree.

BEST SEAT IN THE HOUSE

Jesus comes to the tree and invites himself to the house of Zacchaeus, a tax collector. "Come down! I am coming over" (Luke 19:5, my paraphrase). This was a scandalous thing to do. Jesus was going to share time and space with this reviled member of society. Jesus has gone from using a parable to depict the acceptance of tax collectors in the kingdom to demonstrating the same by sharing a meal with Zacchaeus. This is another beautiful depiction of the gospel reaching the outcasts of society and of Jesus searching for one lost person. Even tax collectors matter to Jesus. Those shunned by religious people have an audience with Jesus and entrance into the kingdom. The rich ruler who Jesus encountered was unable to part with his wealth and so be counted in the kingdom (Mark 10:17-22), but Zacchaeus makes the decision to give half of everything to the poor and to make restitution to those he has cheated (Luke 19:8). His entire life is being made new. This newness was not only in his relationship with God, but also his relationship with his community.

Restoration is never intended to heal only an individual; when one life is truly restored, it distributes that wholeness in the lives of those near to them.

In the previous chapter of Luke's Gospel, Jesus tells a parable about a tax collector being made right because of the posture of his heart. Now as Jesus walks along the road we see him demonstrate what he was just teaching. Luke wants his readers to be aware of the connection between restoration and mercy. In the parable, the tax collector entered the temple to be made right, and now Jesus pursues Zacchaeus. Sometimes there is a cry for mercy from the side of the road, and other times Mercy comes to the base of the tree in which you are hiding.

The person who used to be cruel and harsh with his neighbors is evaporating before the eyes of the onlookers. Zacchaeus might have climbed the tree as a way of escape, but when Jesus calls for him to come down, something in him changes. Restoration and mercy are intertwined and cannot be separated. When we pray for one, the other is active in our lives as well.

GOD RESTORES MY SOUL

There are some passages of Scripture that are familiar even if your upbringing wasn't inside a community of faith. Sporting events have a poster of John 3:16 somewhere in the stands, and Psalm 23 has found its way into even the most secular of minds. There is a line from that psalm that has become one of the most important simple prayers of my life: "He restores my soul" (Psalm 23:3).

Time and chance happen to us all; there are seasons when life is filled with joy and celebration and others when life is bitter and harsh. I can vividly remember getting a phone call from my wife when we first found out that our pregnancy with our third child, Kenzie Grace, was going to be a challenge. The options were foggy, but all signs were directing us to either a pregnancy resulting in a special needs child or her not making it to term. I felt like the air had been sucked out of my lungs. I couldn't breathe and my mind was flooded with fear and worry.

I immediately doubled over, and uncontrollable tears flowed out of my cupped hands that grasped my face. I snuck out of the office and managed to get home before Nicole arrived, and I sank onto the couch in the living room and prayed the most powerful simple prayer of my life: "Please!" I couldn't find any other words, and in a very powerful way felt as if I didn't need any. God knew exactly what I was communicating and was present. I couldn't feel it, but God was there, and I was sure he wouldn't run out on me. Sitting on my couch, I didn't fully know what was ahead for our family, but I knew that we were not alone. Once again I was reminded that sometimes the most powerful of prayers are not high on word count.

Simple prayers provided a way to be fully present to God when I wasn't fully me.

It's been two years since my wife and I lost our daughter Kenzie Grace. The pain of losing a child is more painful than I can capture with words. We endured the anxiety of a high-risk pregnancy, the finality of broken dreams, and the lingering ache of our shattered hearts when she passed. We walked hand in hand into the same hospital where we welcomed our other two beautiful children knowing that the outcome would be tragically different. There we struggled through the grueling delivery of a still, silent, and lifeless baby girl. It is deafening how loud the silence can scream in those moments. I just bowed my head and cried and cried. There were no words to say, no prayers to pray. Our hearts were in utter ruin. There are moments when it's hard to pray. There are seasons when it is hard to be present in prayer, when you feel like God has been absent.

God hadn't come through as we had expected. We prayed and believed and believed and prayed. We wanted to be trusted with her life for longer than the six months that we were given, and the reality that we were called to be Kenzie's parents for a short time is still difficult to comprehend.

There are some things that no one can prepare for. Sometimes there are no classes to take or books to read. Sometimes you have to pave the road as you walk. No one could have prepared me to walk a graveyard and select the final resting place for my daughter or given me the strength to choose a casket for her to be buried in. I have heard of supernatural grace and always thought a euphoric sensation would accompany it. I now know the moments that require that type of grace are moments when you are unable to feel anything and the grace just keeps you standing. You are graced simply to remain.

How do you pray when your heart is broken and your dreams have been shattered? You pray simple prayers. Simple prayers have been part of my spiritual rehabilitation. When I couldn't find many words, I was able to cling to simple prayers.

It has been two years, and we are still picking up the pieces. There are stretches when this all feels like another lifetime or a really bad dream and other times when it feels like this happened just weeks ago. There have been a few occasions when I will see a child that looks around the age Kenzie would be, and the next breath is hard to find. I need a grace to remain. In that moment, I take a breath and pray simply, *God restores my soul.* I let it echo throughout my heart and mind.

Simple prayer helped me put one foot in front of the other. It allowed me to make a move toward God and know that my words mattered. They weren't thrown together or offered half-heartedly; they were all that I had to offer. There were moments as I prayed this simple prayer when I could sense a new grace for that moment that wasn't there previously. There were other moments when I didn't want to move forward or when it felt like it was too much to bear, and this simple prayer kept me in the game.

God, restore my soul.

PRACTICING THESE SIMPLE
PRAYERS OF RESTORATION

Simple prayer is about getting us to move beyond our words and to enter into a deeper intimacy with God by way of the Spirit. A beautiful phrase in Romans 8 mentions that the Spirit groans in intercession in a way that is "too deep for words" or, as I like to imagine it, beyond our language (Romans 8:26). This idea of prayer being beyond our words captures well what simple prayers have meant in my life. I have many times used my words as a distraction for myself—and truthfully for God too: *Perhaps if I pray this way, God will ignore what is actually going on.* Praying simple prayers requires honesty.

Have mercy. The road to renewal is found in the mercy of God. One of the most powerful parts of the Jesus Prayer is the request for mercy. The request finds its biblical origins from these parables in Luke's Gospel. Often the Jesus Prayer has been condensed even further to this prayer—*have mercy*. Powerfully, the revelation of mercy requires that we ask for it. We demonstrate humility in acknowledging to ourselves and to God that only his mercy will restore us. Where do you need to experience the relief that is only found in the mercy of God? Allow this prayer to be the posture you live from and in turn be a grace that you receive.

Take a moment and pray this simple prayer. Give yourself some space to pray for a few minutes. Don't rush through it. The deeper works of the Spirit are not done in microwaveable moments but in the lingering. As you linger and pray, his mercy will appear. It might seem like levity to your mind or a feeling of relief. It might even remind you of a situation where mercy is needed. For example, political seasons bring the worst out of us. They divide and often appeal to the worst parts of who we are; those are moments when a cry for mercy on behalf of a nation is a prophetic act of compassion. When mercy comes, it might not do anything to us that will change us externally, but just as the tax collector walked out of the temple with mercy beaming on the inside, you too can feel the renewing grace that mercy offers.

Restore my soul. There is a good chance that we are all walking around wounded. We have the scars of hurts that have accumulated over time. Some of the wounds are fresh and leave us walking with a limp, and others feel like you have been holding hands with your woundedness—it has begun to feel like an old friend.

This simple prayer can be a prophetic prayer in a painful season. Maybe you find yourself in a place where you long for restoration. Take hold of this simple prayer and pray it with a courage that assures you that while restoration might not be here yet, it is coming. This prayer is a reminder that God alone is faithful and able to restore. When life and even death have left us breaking apart, this simple prayer is one to cling to.

He restores my soul. Allow that statement to flood your mind with courage to remain. You may not be on the other side just yet, but the Good Shepherd will work tenderly if you have been hurt severely.

Are you in the middle of a dark season where you can't seem to find a light switch to turn on? If you are broken, God will be faithful to put you back together. He is merciful, and in his mercy he restores. More than likely it will take more time than you want. Remain in him; restoration is a process. While you may feel lost, he will find you. Jesus comes after those who are disconnected and on the borders. He came to Zacchaeus while he was in a tree. He heard the cry for mercy from a blind beggar on the road, and the tax collector in the temple was made right. Our hearts can be restored, and it all begins with a cry for mercy.

7

Simple Words to Pray

*The only thing left is the simplicity of the soul in
God—or, better, the Simplicity of God.*

THOMAS MERTON

I am a Cubs fan. This short statement tells you so much about me. It tells you that I am loyal. It tells you that I have the ability to believe in the unseen. To be able to faithfully root for a team that went 108 years between World Series wins requires an incredible amount of loyalty. I still remember my first pilgrimage to Wrigley Field. I entered the turnstiles beneath the signature red sign facing the corner of Addison and Clark and felt like I was stepping through the cornfields with Kevin Costner and Ray Liotta in *Field of Dreams*. I was immediately transported to a different time and different place. Over the years I have learned that there are certain words and phrases that have special meaning to Cubs fans. Words that seem innocuous to most are near and dear to our hearts. Words paint pictures and invite us into experiences. For Cubs fans, words like *brick* and *ivy* bring a smile to our faces—and on the other side of the coin, words like *curse* and *Bartman* send chills down our spines.

The words we say matter and how we say them matter a great deal. Simple prayers are powerful because of that fact. Our words are loaded with our emotions and experiences, and when we use them we are painting pictures for people to examine and inviting them into experiences.

THE ORIGINAL SIMPLE PRAYER

This idea of praying short phrases or words is not new. For as long as people have been praying, they have wanted their prayers to take them beyond the surface and plunge them deep into the presence of God. The goal of prayer is intimacy, and true intimacy doesn't require many words. Sometimes our words can ruin a moment; after all, they are only words. Intimacy is discovered beyond language. It is why we say things like, "I can't even begin to describe" or "I can't seem to find the words" when life feels larger than the containers our words create.

For years I wanted to experience depth in my relationship with God, but I tried to achieve it with words. In doing so I sacrificed intimacy. My tradition celebrates long, loud prayers and treats the opposite as a junior-varsity type of spirituality. The thought crept in that the more eloquent and profound my vocabulary could be, the better received my prayer would be in the heavenly courts. What I found was the complete opposite. While my prayers seemed to impress the people around me, inwardly I knew they were hollow. They were the prayer version of whitewashed tombs. I needed some fresh perspective, and I was able to find it in the Christian mystics.

Two important mystics were some of the first to pray simple prayers. The first, John Cassian (AD 360–435), was born in present-day Romania and in his youth traveled to a monastery in Bethlehem to live an ascetic life. One of the principles of Cassian spirituality is that the monastic life should serve as an entrance into the kingdom of God, into eternal life, which can be experienced in the present. Prayer offers us a transcendental experience if we are able to press beyond the distractions. Cassian believed that the monk ought to be attentive to God alone; this attention produces a union with God that has several forms. In his work *Conferences*, Cassian introduces the Eastern monastic practice of *monologistos*—a prayer that consists of a single phrase or word. The Jesus Prayer is perhaps the most popular monologistos.

The second mystic is John Climacus (AD 579–649), who wrote the spiritual classic *Ladder of Divine Ascent* and found the ideal prayer to be a monologistos. Climacus writes, "Do not launch out into long discourses that fritter away your mind in efforts for eloquence. One word alone spoken by the Publican touched God's mercy; a single word full of faith saved the Good Thief. Prolixity in prayer often fills the mind with images and distracts it, while often one single word draws into recollection." These words redirected my prayer life.

The single-word prayer was not to be an accompaniment to but the very essence of one's breath. What is offered is not a ritualistic prayer but a rhythm of life to enter into. A monologistos serves the soul in the same manner that breathing serves the body, providing strength and vitality. The simple prayer serves as a source of life in the midst of life.

The Jesus Prayer is a traditional monologistos, but there are also ways that we can take this method and embrace new words as simple prayers.

BEYOND THE MUSIC

I love the Hebrew wisdom literature. The honest and raw emotion of it appeals to me. The rhythm of the writing is smooth and abrupt, sometimes in the same moment. The crown jewel of the genre is the Psalms. Eugene Peterson offers this insight: "Most Christians for most of the centuries have learned to pray by praying the Psalms. The Hebrews, with several centuries of a head start on us in matters of prayer and worship, provided us with this prayer book that gives us a language adequate for responding to the God who speaks to us." As a pastor, Peterson began paraphrasing the Psalms for his congregants, who he was guiding in prayer development. His exercise grew into what we now know as *The Message* translation of the Bible. It began in the Psalms for the purpose of helping people learn to pray.

The Psalms were used in public worship in Israel as well as for private devotions. They show us how intimate and free our relationship with God can be as we share every thought and feeling with him. Among the thousands of words that the Scriptures offer us to guide our prayers, there are a few that I want us to consider and embrace as examples of a modern-day monologistos—a new simple prayer in the vein of the mystics.

PAUSE AND REFLECT

Pause. Rest. Take a break and change modes. Breathe deeply. The word *selah* is used seventy-one times in the Psalms and is used to create space to pause. Its exact meaning remains unclear, but most agree that it denotes a musical interlude or transition. The root word means to "lift up," which leads some to believe that it also marks the climax in the music where the voices and instruments are to lift up in praise to God.

When I think of *selah*, I think of a time to pause and reflect. Space created to breathe deeply, an opportunity to lift our hearts to God in worship. When we read the text, we don't actually say "selah," we just acknowledge it with a pause.

Sometimes the most powerful prayers are filled with a pause. Have you ever had a moment when the honesty of your words met the grandness of who God is, and it required space? Those are selah moments—moments when moving on doesn't honor the present. When the writer of the Psalms used *selah*, it was to create that needed space. It is to say, "That was good" or "This needs to be considered a little longer," or perhaps it is a revelation or truth that you need to sit with for a moment. Take a full stop.

This practice directly opposes the ways many of us construct our daily lives. We move between conversations with ease. Think about how many text conversations you are currently having (full disclosure, I have three going while I am writing this section). We communicate more now than ever, but I wonder whether we ever allow the series of words and phrases to settle into our souls. We have the fatigue of being with everyone and the pain of potentially never being with anyone. This simple prayer of selah is to create space for us to breathe, to enjoy the moment we are in before it turns into a memory in the rearview mirror.

We have all seen groups gathered together for coffee with their faces glowing from the screens of their smart phones: more connected, yet further apart. When we pray, this happens as well. Our words come one after the other, and once we have exhausted our words, we are finished praying. No pause. No moment to let it settle in deep. I think we pray because we believe in its power functionally, but we lose the moments of formation that can only happen with reflection. Simple prayers help us embrace these selah moments. Sometimes the silence makes the music—and the prayer—all the more powerful.

This word has become a prayerful reminder to take in the moments as they come. There are times when the best response to an experience is to simply pray, "Selah."

I am reminded whenever I look at Timehop how quickly the time passes. This app is a beautiful reminder that time flies—enjoy each day because before you know it, you will be living it only in memory. My kids are growing up, and *selah* is a word I hold on to when the pressures of work seem to invade the space needed for quality time with them. Selah.

The pause brings comfort and peace in the midst of the chaos. It brings what needs to be seen into focus. The email isn't more important than reading with my kids before bed.

TO KNOW AND BE KNOWN

Another word that is powerful to pray is *know*. The Hebrew word *yada* is translated "know." It is used to describe covenantal relationships as well as to communicate intimacy. Knowledge comes with a responsibility. The word is used to talk about the sexual bond between Adam and Eve and is also used to describe Eve's desire to know good and evil. A weight comes when we know something. For example, when God directs his people to separate from a particular people group or false god, he doesn't want his people to *know* those other gods. Knowledge is a powerful tool.

The story of the Garden of Eden paints for us a story of knowing, not a scientific treatise focused on chronological frameworks or an attempt to time-stamp the universe. Genesis is the beginning of the story. It introduces us to the Creator and invites us into the rhythm and order of God's world. It offers a picture of the relationship between God and humanity. It is and will always be initiated by God. The story provides examples of human interaction with God. Genesis 2:16-17 is not just a warning for Adam and Eve to not eat from the tree but a reminder that we have all eaten from the tree. Genesis gives us a window into the human story. Scripture is most powerful when we see ourselves in the narrative. Adam and Eve are not alone in choosing to go their own way and, in the process, moving further from God. Sometimes we bite off what is too difficult to swallow.

Being known is a weighty thing. It requires trust and a willingness to be vulnerable. It's a paradox that we live in a culture that is connected and dominated by social media, yet we have a difficult time being vulnerable. We say everything and nothing at the same time. Vulnerability is much less calculated than the way we have become used to living. I recently went to a baseball game (yes, a Cubs game) where a group of twentysomethings spent the better part of the first three innings taking selfies. Every photo taken was followed by a group vote deciding whether to post or delete the photo. It was exhausting and sad. It had become more important to report about the great time they were having at the game than to truly enjoy the game and each other's company.

We only display the best moments for others to browse and discard the less-than-perfect moments. We create personas rather than developing deeper levels of vulnerability. I have found that I have to be careful with social media. It is easy to try to contour our lives to look their best online. It is a sad day when we are more concerned with the "likes" a post gets than we are with being fully present in the moment. It is great to catalog our experiences, but not at the expense of actually enjoying the moment. I have decided that not everything I do will be posted online. Some moments have to be sacred. Vulnerability is best experienced face to face, not face to screen.

I am not sure that Scripture offers us a more vulnerable figure than David. David's life is filled with grand triumph and tragic regret. Yet the grace of God allows him still to be known by God. Our faults don't erase us from God's memory or his heart. There is a beauty in the fact that God knows David, and regardless of where he finds himself, God is with him. Psalm 139 captures this beautifully:

> Where shall I go from your Spirit?
>   Or where shall I flee from your presence?
> If I ascend to heaven, you are there!
>   If I make my bed in Sheol, you are there!
> If I take the wings of the morning
>   and dwell in the uttermost parts of the sea,
> even there your hand shall lead me,
>   and your right hand shall hold me. (Psalm 139:7-10)

To be known is to never be alone. Ask any couple that gets married and blends their lives together. You know that person much differently than you did when you didn't share an address or a box of cereal. Exposure is part of intimacy. Everywhere there are people in relationships who engage physically but have not exposed their hearts to one another. The beauty of intimacy comes in mutuality: you know me and you are known by me. When our relationships lack this critical portion, they are the equivalent of houses built on shifting sand.

We take these same fractured, relational rhythms and transpose them into our spiritually. We want to have encounters with God without any knowledge. We don't want the responsibility of remaining that comes with knowing. One of the things I love about David is that he is riddled with sin (like all of us; we just sin differently) and he is aware that God knows him. God desires not only to know but also to be known. An assurance comes when we pray, *You know me*. And we gain confidence that we can also know God.

The apostle Paul desired to know Christ, to share in his sufferings, and so in some way to experience the resurrection (Philippians 3:10-11). The suffering of the cross is always the prequel to the power of the resurrection. We have to pass through one to be able to walk out of the other. Suffering allows us to know what we otherwise would not have known.

SOMEBODY SAVE ME!

When the crowd hears that Jesus is coming to town, they line the streets waving palm branches and saying, "Hosanna!" The people lining the parade route are the same people who have heard the teachings and seen the miracles. They are all in with Jesus. These are also the same people who live under the rule of the Romans, and there is part of them that is not simply welcoming Jesus with incredible hospitality. This is a coronation. Perhaps he will be a king like David—one who left the people chanting and singing songs of his military exploits. There would be time in the future to reprise their lyrics, so for now a simple cry of "Hosanna"— "save us"—will suffice. What they didn't know was that Jesus was not overthrowing any government; he was inaugurating a kingdom. The people wanted to be saved, but only in the way that they envisioned.

I have often stood among them. I have lifted my voice crying out for salvation but hoping it would be done just as I prescribed. "Jesus, save me from me, but do precisely as I suggest."

When we embrace the word *hosanna* as a prayer, it reminds us that we need to be saved and that there is only one who can do it. It also reminds us that the type of saving we need extends beyond the present moment. "Hosanna" becomes a more powerful prayer when we think about it through the lens of the bigger picture: the kingdom of God has come, and the saving that is taking place is greater than I was even aware. When I pray this simple prayer of hosanna, it invites me to surrender fully to Jesus. It relinquishes control and places my trust and hope in Jesus.

Hosanna is a reminder that the King entered town on a donkey. This wasn't a military brigade; it was borrowed livestock. When you pray this simple prayer, pray with the kingdom of God in mind: *Save us in the spirit and the might of the kingdom.* This prayer has served me as a reorientation. When I want to prescribe what my rescue should look like, I am reminded to trust in the King. I do not trust a king who overthrows governments or wins elections but a King who overcomes death and the grave. That is the kind of King who can indeed save me.

PRACTICING THESE SIMPLE WORDS TO PRAY

In keeping with the Christian mystics, these single-word simple prayers are powerful for us. Like all simple prayers they create space for the Spirit to commune with us as we pray. This requires space. There are moments in our lives when we know that too much speech is harmful. Each of these simple prayers is designed to make us pause, settle in, and return. The pause is the moment when we acknowledge that we could move on from this moment but make the decision not to. Prayer is retreating from the natural world to find ourselves when we are with God. Each of these words can serve as a simple prayer. They remind us that some moments invite us into moments of pause.

Selah. I am finding that my life is getting more and more full, often with good things–kingdom things even—but even so, there are moments when the prayer of my life needs to be a simple prayer of selah.

When life is too good to rush by, simply pray *selah*. When there is news that is overwhelming and it is hard to find the next breath, *selah*. Life can easily be lived and not enjoyed. We can move from conversation to conversation and not allow ourselves to be known.

You know me. To be known by God is more than saying that God is aware of us; it is to say that God desires to inhabit every detail of our lives. God is not looking for a social media relationship with us, a relationship from afar. A need for intimacy is woven into us, and we all wander until we find our home in God. I remember watching the sitcom *Cheers* when I was younger. I loved when Norm would cross the threshold of the bar, and everyone greeted him with a loud, "Norm." He was beloved, he was known. Take a moment and pray this simple prayer: *You know me.* Allow each repetition of this prayer to provide more and more assurance to your heart that you are indeed known by God. Your actions cannot undo this and you cannot earn it. You are not known as the sum of your skills or achievements. You are not embraced by the love of God because you have accumulated wealth or possess status. You are known because you are the beloved of God.

Hosanna. The cry to be saved comes from a place of desperation. This cry testifies that the present isn't what it could or should be. It asserts that the one praying isn't the one who can save. Like those crying out along the road as Jesus rides into town, I want to be rescued—even if I may not fully know from what.

8

Simple Prayer of Finding Your Way

Yet not what I will, but what you will.

PRAYER OF A SURRENDERING SAVIOR

Your kingdom come, your will be done.
On earth as it is in heaven.

THE LORD'S PRAYER

He must increase, but I must decrease.

PRAYER OF JOHN IN THE DESERT

While we are finding our way, we need to make sure we aren't actually losing it. The prodigal son is a picture of this. He left home to find freedom and live without responsibility and restraint. After a period of wild living, his inheritance was squandered, his newly found friends were nowhere to be found, and the young Jewish prodigal was sitting in a pigpen. Can you imagine the filth and the smell? The low point of the story comes as he begins to envy the servants at his father's house. The road home was more difficult than the road out of town. The runaway son would have to see his father face-to-face, and their last conversation had been when he told his father that he was as good as dead to him. The long road home was filled with a rehearsal of the "I was wrong" speech.

Maybe you have disappointed those you loved. Perhaps you have run away and vowed never to come back. Did you ever have arguments with someone and after the yelling a silence entered the relationship that lasted for months or years? Maybe you befriended people who left you in worse shape than when they met you. If we are honest, we have all had moments where we felt like we were alone in a pen filled with swine.

If we are honest, we have all given that "I was wrong" speech a time or two.

I can imagine the anxiety of the prodigal son growing with each step closer to home. Passers-by would have heard him rehearsing his speech. "Father, I have sinned against heaven and before you. I am no longer worthy to be called your son. Treat me as one of your hired servants" (Luke 15:18-19). The Scriptures are most powerful when we can find ourselves in them. When we read the story, we can see our story intertwined. The story of the lost son is powerful because at some time we can all see ourselves in the reflection of the son who wandered away. We have all traded our position in the family for short-lived memories that become long-term pain. Jesus tells this parable as part of a series of parables about lost things and the joy that comes when they are found. The pain of loss is overshadowed in the light of being found.

I love the way Jesus tells the story: "But while he was still a long way off, his father saw him and felt compassion, and ran and embraced him and kissed him" (Luke 15:20). Parables frame supernatural realities through natural stories, and in this story we are given an example of the way the heavenly Father responds to us coming home. He feels compassion; he embraces us and kisses us. All of this happens while the son is still covered in filth from his escapades. We never have to get cleaned up before coming home.

Yet it is easy to feel just the opposite when it comes to prayer—that we have to get it all right before making our way to the Father. But when we decide to come home, we simply need to come. The rehearsed speech never makes it out of our mouths in the midst of the Father's greeting and embrace. It is hard to explain why you should be loved when you are being loved.

PRAYING FOR ALIGNMENT

Prayer is the vehicle that brings us to the Father, and embracing simple prayer is to take a step toward knowing and being known. Simple prayer is about creating space for us to hear and be heard. Most of us focus on the being heard part of prayer. We want the right words to say so that we get the right result. In the Western world we pray for outcomes. In the mind of Jesus we should pray for alignment: *Not what I will, but what you will.*

I have always been intrigued by the theme of the garden in the biblical story. We begin in a garden called Eden, where we are introduced to the Creator and his evening strolls alongside Adam and Eve. This picture of a relationship with God undisturbed by sin is an encounter we have since longed for. A garden is also where we later find Jesus praying a simple and gut-wrenching prayer.

"Abba, Father, all things are possible for you. Remove this cup from me. Yet not what I will, but what you will" (Mark 14:36).

Jesus offers a simple prayer in the most troubling of times. Simple prayers are not dependent on simple moments to be effective. Jesus has known his mission on earth is to be a sacrifice, but the reality is almost more than he can bear. Jesus is aware of how close he is to the end. He has brought a few close friends along to pray with him. Jesus was hoping his friends would be able to help him bear the weight of this together, but they all fell asleep. When those around you are sleeping, it is good to know that God isn't. When those you hoped could help you bear the burden fail you, God is still wide awake.

Jesus' words are intriguing and extremely honest. It is hard for most people to be acquainted with the idea that Jesus was fully human. It is easier to digest the deity of Jesus than it is to accept the humanity of Jesus. Deep in our hearts we want to be rescued by God. It becomes difficult to see salvation come from a person who is looking for a way out. Make no mistake about it, Jesus was asking for a Plan B. The dark cloud of death lurked around the corner, and Jesus was looking for any way out. The Messiah wasn't certain that he could drink the cup. Haven't you been there before? Where the calling on your life seemed to fade away in a moment of pressure? If we are living our lives for ourselves, those prayers sound much different than Jesus' prayer. We pray for the cup to be taken. We acknowledge that we don't want to go through this, and then we look for a side exit. Jesus isn't praying the prayer of convenience; he is praying the prayer of surrender.

He is clear with his desires but still remains submitted to the Father. The true heart of surrender is found in a person who is willing to remain submitted even in their darkest hour. Jesus in his humanity teaches us what it means to live for the kingdom in the face of death.

I remember my grandmother telling us that there was a point in my grandfather's final days battling cancer that she began to pray that the Lord would take him home. I couldn't comprehend that prayer. It was the opposite prayer that my heart was praying. I wanted my Poppy to be healed. I wanted cancer to be defeated and for life to get back to the way it was. Her prayer directly opposed that. As I think about that now, her prayer was a version of Jesus' prayer from the garden. She had resolved in her heart that her desires would align with the will of the Father. Those are prayers that are simple in structure but far from easy.

Praying this prayer reminds me to submit my desires to the one who is Lord over all. Even in the face of death the decision to align with the will of God is always a good decision. It will not be easy or convenient, but it is best. *Not what I will, but what you will.*

KINGDOM COME

The disciples wanted to learn how to pray, so they asked Jesus for help. Jesus provided them with a simple rhythm that you and I now know as the Lord's Prayer. Its structure may be compact, but the Lord's Prayer provides words and phrases that can be encountered in deep and powerful ways. The prayer gives us direction on living with others in a posture of forgiveness, beginning with a posture toward heaven. Perhaps the most powerful line in the prayer is "Your kingdom come, your will be done, on earth as it is in heaven" (Matthew 6:10).

In other words, "Above all else, let your kingdom be established in our midst, here below as it is above." The prayer is for the rule and reign of God to be set up in this moment as it has been for all eternity in celestial places. This simple prayer is far more powerful when I think of Jesus in the garden praying for his life to be spared. Even unto death he was committed to establishing the kingdom of God here and now.

When Jesus was doubled over in the garden wanting another option, his prayer did not end with despair but refocused his eyes on the Father once again. His flesh was weak, but his spirit never lost its vision. Without vision we may perish, but with it we can stare down death.

My friend Chris Maxwell is a wonderful writer, and for years he has had a devotional blog called *Another Day Along the Way*. I love the picture those words craft. Our lives are lived in sequence, and the sum of our experiences equals who we are and who we are becoming. Each day there are conversations and moments for us to dance with the Divine. We sometimes lead and other times are being led in this dance. Some songs are fast and filled with energy, and other songs are slow and invite us into a melody of rest. Life is a beautiful collection of moments and memories. I especially find this to be true with my kids. Every day seems ordinary, but each day is filled with distinction. I try to live with the mindset, "I will have a lot of days that resemble today but I never get this day again." This keeps me present.

I had the opportunity a few years ago to hear Reggie Joiner talk about the days we have with each of our kids and how we lose one each day. It was illustrated with a jar of 6,570 marbles—one for every day of your child's life before their eighteenth birthday. It was a very tangible image of what Moses wrote in Psalm 90: "Teach us to number our days" (Psalm 90:12). I will never forget the feeling I had when looking at that jar. Every day I am losing a marble. These moments must be lived in a way that makes each memory count. Each day I want each of my children to hear certain things. I want them to have certain prayers prayed over them, into them, and for them—prayers they connect with that will stay with them when they leave home. I have to take the moments in life to teach them to see the spiritual all around them. And sometimes we learn a lot just by opening doors.

OPEN DOORS

One of the things I love most about being a dad is the teaching moments that arise in the rhythm of normal routines with each kid. These moments mold and shape who they are and who they are becoming. My oldest son, Caden, started kindergarten this year, and according to a poster I saw many years ago, this is the year he will learn everything he will need to know. Understandably, I feel some pressure to get it right this year.

I remember being Caden's age and my dad teaching me to hold the door open for people. It was a simple lesson. When you get to a door, open it, but before you enter look around to see if there is anyone coming along for whom you can hold the door. This simple gesture has become a foundational thought in my leadership. Each day we have the opportunity to "hold doors" for people. We can create space for others to grow and become exactly who God designed them to be, or we can be focused solely on where we are going and what we need to do. Great leadership requires an element of hospitality. Leadership is about creating space and opportunities for others and then caring for those you have welcomed in.

Holding a door is a simple act of service, a symbolic gesture that you value and honor the person you are allowing to go in front of you. Doing this will delay your arrival, but the beauty is that you will never arrive alone. When we pray for the kingdom of God to be realized here as it is in the heavenly realms, we are opening a door for heaven to enter. This prayer revitalizes our current location while uniting our hearts with the desire of the kingdom for the world.

Jesus modeled this way of life for his disciples and then encouraged them to do the same. The kingdom of God is most powerful when it is not an idea swirling in our minds but is active in our daily lives. We may not bring God's kingdom into existence—only he can do that—but we can invite it, try to recognize it, and participate in it in everyday life.

DECREASE FOR INCREASE

Jesus had a cousin named John. They were only months apart in age and their ministries were connected. In utero John leapt at the coming of Jesus, and as a man in the desert he exuberantly declared the coming of the Messiah. John's following was growing. People trekked toward the outskirts of town to see a man who wore the skins of animals and ate bugs and honey. His message was clear: Repent, the kingdom of heaven is near. He was paving the way for the ministry of Jesus. John knew his role and understood that his mission was to allow Jesus to increase and John to fade away.

"He must increase, but I must decrease" (John 3:30). John reveals his character in this simple statement, which flowed out of an honest place in his soul. This is the downward mobility required in the kingdom. The kingdom of God will always be in opposition to the empires of this world. There are moments when the empire the kingdom opposes is a superpower like Rome, but frequently, when the kingdom is opposing an empire the empire is you. The temptation is strong to hoard power and keep the attention of those around you with spectacular exploits. Yet there is a direct way to handle this growing ego and hunger for more: become less. In the face of the crowd growing—and with John's message now getting the Messiah's endorsement—John makes the calculated decision to become less so that Jesus will become more. If there is ever a prayer that helps us find our way, it's this one. Jesus taught his followers that the way to gain life was to lose it; John knew that. He knew that he would fulfill the purpose set for him if he faded into the background. This is not a prayer for the faint of heart. John is not abdicating leadership or promoting lethargy. It is quite the opposite; he is fully aware of what he is doing. He is leading others to focus more fully on Jesus. His role is to prepare the way of the Lord. I like to think of John as the opening act and Jesus as the headliner.

There are moments when our prayers are not informing God of something, they are reminding us of what really matters. This is a critical prayer for us to pray. If you are leading anything, you will need a continual reminder of who and what truly matters. I can slip into moments where productivity overshadows people. I am terrible at disengaging from my phone. I catch myself far too frequently looking over at it during conversations in which I should be fully attentive to the person I am with. My thoughts drift to what I should be doing rather than being fully devoted to the present moment. I have to be reminded of the goals and the purpose of my life. Production is a portion but people are the focus. That must steer my life. Simple prayers help remind me of what matters most.

This simple prayer responds to the ever-elusive question of our purpose. The Westminster Catechism says that the chief goal of humanity is to glorify God and enjoy him forever. Our greatest potential for enjoyment is to see that God is glorified. For this to be a reality in our lives, we must not seek glory that is not ours. This prayer of John counterbalances the pride that easily grows in the dark places of our hearts. Of all the things that we could feel designed for, we are first created to follow Jesus. After that, we concern ourselves only with how to express that calling.

My life expresses my devotion to Jesus in a variety of ways. My purpose becomes convoluted when I try to master the expressions without first understanding that my primary calling is as a disciple. When we let ourselves be driven by any purpose other than following Jesus and expressing our devotion to him in all areas of life, we miss out on our life's true significance. This is not a diminished life but one lived in alignment and congruence with our design, and it is filled with wonder and significance. Isn't that all that we have ever truly wanted? John had a firm grasp of that. He knew the calling and direction of his life, and he had the courage to live it out.

He must increase, I must decrease.

Our prayers are powerful when they are displayed in our lives and not merely heard. John's life amplified his prayer. He was aware of his assignment, and his life and prayers declared the same message. Sometimes simple prayers are found in simple obedience. There are moments when our most true prayers are actions, as in John's example. If he had made this statement about decreasing so that Jesus would increase and then continued to try to build his following, it would have been a lie. His obedience was seen in his decision to move to a lesser position. His life was louder than his prayers. He brought his prayers to life with his actions. Are you willing to live louder than your prayers? If so, you will find your prayers to be far more powerful.

SIMPLY JIM

When I was two my mom married a man for whom I will forever be grateful. Jim is a man of character and integrity. He has taught me about being a husband and a father and what it means to serve the Lord. I certainly would not be who I am today without my dad. My birth father gave up rights to me when I was very young. As a father, I am not sure how or why he made that decision, but even though he abandoned me, Jim adopted me. I have lived my life between the reality of being loved and being forgotten. My dad Jim decided thirty-three years ago not just to say that he loved me but to live out that love. It has made it easier to forget being forgotten.

This reassurance happened in the simple moments of playing catch; it was heard in the corrective tone of his voice when I had stepped out of bounds. It was the grace he gave me when I got in an accident days after getting my license. It was seeing him smile when I would win in sports, but more than that, his smile as I navigated my life's transitions—graduations, wedding day, becoming a dad. Our conversations may be simple, but their impact has been significant. I know I am loved not because I heard words of affection, but because those words were also accompanied by a steady life that brought those words into being.

PRACTICING THESE SIMPLE
PRAYERS OF FINDING YOUR WAY

The simple prayers of finding our way are there to help us remember that life isn't about us. We cannot only accept Jesus as Savior and not allow him to be Lord as well. These simple prayers help us find our way home in the kingdom of God. Each of these prayers serves to combat our ego and the ambition that can creep into our hearts as followers of Jesus.

Not what I will, but what you will. We have a great saying around the office: "You get paid to make decisions!" It is truly empowering, but it is not permission to make decisions outside of the mission and vision of the organization. That would be reckless. Our spiritual life works the same way. We are empowered to live but are reminded that not all choices will be beneficial to us. This simple prayer reminds me that my ability to choose should never move beyond my desire to submit to the will of the King. I have found that I love the idea of Jesus as Savior and friend but have often resented him as King because it meant that I couldn't be in charge. I have found that this simple prayer quiets the ambition in my heart. Do you find yourself struggling with pride and ego? Are you in positions of leadership and have begun to feel your humility slipping away? Lean into this simple prayer and slowly begin to whisper, "Not what I will, but what you will."

This is a dangerous prayer and one that needs to be considered before launching into it. If this prayer is prayed with the heart and mind it will shift the way you view everything. It reframes how you move and position yourself in your career. It changes how you pray for you kids and their futures.

Your kingdom come, your will be done, on earth as it is in heaven. This simple prayer is a cry for realignment and a reminder that the patterns we find ourselves a part of are often not congruent with the order of the kingdom of God. So I often pray this simple prayer in two parts.

The first part is to declare that the kingdom is coming! In the face of the world unraveling before our eyes at times, the kingdom of God is near! The psalmist reminds us that his nearness to us is for our good (Psalm 73:28). This simple prayer is for the will and way of God to be realized.

The second part is a powerful declaration, "on earth as it is in heaven." Some translations read "in earth." I love the picture that provides us. Regardless of how we would like to be perceived, the truth is that we are dirt. We are earthen vessels and simple jars of clay, but we house the mysterious and wonderful treasure of Christ within us. This prayer invites the way of heaven to be the way *of* and *in* earth. I want heaven to be realized here, but often the prerequisite is that it must first be realized in me. Pray that line using both "on" and "in" language. Allow the request to be made with your heart. Great moves of the Spirit begin in simple prayers and then are lived out in lives guided by obedience.

This simple prayer is a prayer of lordship. Jesus is the King and there are no rebuttals in heaven. He is the first and final word. In the kingdom of God we can pray a prayer of surrender and a prayer of exaltation simultaneously.

He must increase, but I must decrease. Self-promotion has become normative in our society. Most of us have social media accounts, and if we aren't careful they move from tools to document and create to instruments of propaganda used to peddle our own brand. I must admit I love it when I get a new follower or friend request. It does something to my shallow heart that wants to get noticed and desires approval. Because I know this, I have to censor what I put on these platforms. I want to be careful that my accounts don't become places to exalt my life for the world to see and be in awe of. I have friends who will text me if I put something egocentric on one of my social media profiles. It is one matter to document, another to want to incite others to admire me.

This simple prayer can serve as a reminder of our purpose. John the Baptist had a crowd, a following, and he knew that the crowd following him needed to be certain that Jesus was the one on whom they should place their focus. If you feel your life becoming more about you and your social media footprint, this may be a good time to pray this prayer. Maybe you are in a season of success and you need to temper that with a prayer reminding you that Jesus is the true focal point.

A FEW WORDS BEFORE WE SAY AMEN

I had a professor in college who began each prayer where his previous prayer left off. He never began with the traditional salutations. I remember that the first time I heard him pray, I was certain that I had missed the beginning. I was thrown off by the lack of a proper greeting, but over time it became clear to me that he was simply inviting us to join in on a dialogue that was ongoing between him and God. His prayer was less about formality and all about authenticity. It has been over a decade since I had him for a professor, but the genuineness of his prayer has affected me deeply. It is my prayer that simple prayer will do that for you. That it will offer you a window into prayers that are tested throughout the ages and also offer you the freedom to find and craft your own. These prayers are found in the songs that dance around your ears and in the conversations you have with loved ones. They are in the prayers of your children at bedtime. Simple prayers are all around you.

The beauty of simple prayer goes beyond the words to the awareness that comes from knowing that God is listening attentively. Simple prayers aren't fast prayers or phrases used to strong arm God for your benefit. These are prayers of communion. When prayer is hurried or rushed, it loses its ability to be transformative. Transformation doesn't take place at high speeds. Prayer is not an element of a hurried life. These are not magic phrases to get what we want out of God. They are not intended to manipulate God for our own gain. These are prayers intended to lead us to a place of simple purity in our prayers.

My hope is that this invitation to pray simply opens the door for a greater experience with God. Simple prayers invite you inside—no more feeling like you are standing outside of a speakeasy wishing you knew the password. These prayers invite you into deeper and richer moments with God. These moments happen when you decide that prayer is not a grand collection of phrases thrown in God's direction but an opportunity to be honest and at home in the presence of a God who is here and now.

My prayer for you is a simple, *Amen—Let it be so!*

Acknowledgments

Thank you—

Nicole, for challenging me to become the version of myself you have always seen.

Caden, Hailey, and Declan, for reminding me that life is best lived through the eyes of a child.

Mom and Dad, for your unconditional love and support. Dreams are fostered in that environment.

To my family; thank you for believing in me and celebrating each milestone along the way. I am blessed beyond words to be surrounded by you all.

Mark Oestricher, my literary agent, for your encouragement and help to get this dream into the hands of the wonderful people at IVP.

To the SEU community; thank you for providing a place to dream and create alongside some of the finest people I know.

Mark Batterson and Chris Maxwell—your support and guiding voices along the way have been a gift. I am grateful for the private words of support. They mean more than I can truly express.

Chris Owen, for helping me dream this book into existence on your office whiteboard. You are a steady friend who helps call out the best in me.

Robert and Pam Crosby, for being mentoring voices in family, writing, and ministry.

Basil and Kathy Savoie, for being some of the first people who believed in me being a writer. Your words still ring true.

Josh and Becca Turner, for being more than pastors and also dear friends.

Annalee Mutz, Danielle Mitchell, Anastasia Jones Downing, Aeriel Cook, Josh Duke, and J. Joseph Hepler, for reading the early drafts of the book.

And finally, thank you to Eugene Peterson, Henri Nouwen, Dallas Willard, and Richard Foster for introducing me to a way of knowing Jesus and a way of life to follow. Your writings are hopefully easy to see in mine.

Notes

INTRODUCTION

7 *Come to rest*: Henri J. M. Nouwen, *The Way of the Heart: Desert Spirituality and Contemporary Ministry* (New York: Seabury, 1981), 63-64.

1 WHAT IS SIMPLE PRAYER?

12 *one of my favorite book titles*: Brian D. McLaren and Tony Campolo, *Adventures in Missing the Point: How the Culture-Controlled Church Neutered the Gospel* (Grand Rapids: Zondervan, 2003).

16 *Prayers are tools*: Eugene H. Peterson and James N. Watkins, *Answering God: Leader's Guide* (San Francisco: HarperSanFrancisco, 1992), 2.

Most students of the human condition: Ibid., 5.

no one ought to undertake: P. T. Forsyth, *The Soul of Prayer* (London: Charles H. Kelly, 1916), 9; quoted in Simon Chan, *Spiritual Theology: A Systematic Study of the Christian Life* (Downers Grove, IL: InterVarsity Press, 1998), 127.

Theory is not a substitution: Chan, *Spiritual Theology*, 129.

17 *Our Father*: The Lord's Prayer is found in Matthew 6:9-13 and Luke 11:2-4. The last line does not appear in the earliest manuscripts of the New Testament.

19 *all of life is prayer*: Chan, *Spiritual Theology*, 127.

In Simple Prayer: Richard Foster, *Prayer: Finding the Heart's True Home* (San Francisco: HarperCollins, 1992), 9.

2 SIMPLE PRAYER OF THE HEART

26 *monks also left inscriptions*: Billy Kang, *The Jesus Prayer* (Feedbooks, 2011), 9.

26   *In monastic life, prayer is rooted*: Ibid.

27   The *Philokalia*: St. Nikodimos and St. Makarios, *The Philokalia: The Complete Text*, trans. and ed. G. E. H. Palmer, Philip Sherrard, and Kallistos Ware (London: Faber and Faber, 1979).

     The Way of a Pilgrim: Helen Bacovcin, trans., *The Way of a Pilgrim and The Pilgrim Continues His Way* (New York: Doubleday, 1992).

30   *True inner prayer is to stop talking*: Kallistos Ware, "The Power of the Name: The Function of the Jesus Prayer," *Cross Currents* 24 (Summer–Fall 1974): 184-203.

     to the point of full spiritual perception: Taitetsu Unno, "Jesus Prayer and the Nembutsu," *Buddhist-Christian Studies* 22, no. 1 (2002): 93-99.

31   *Meditation is an activation*: Matta Al-Miskin, *Orthodox Prayer Life: The Interior Way* (Crestwood, NY: St. Vladimir's Seminary Press, 2003), 56.

     Contemplation is not beyond the capacity: Ibid., 62.

     It is not concerned with offering verbal prayers: Ibid., 64.

32   *Let all your thoughts be with the Most High*: Thomas á Kempis, *The Imitation of Christ* (London: J. M. Dent & Sons, 1947), 48.

33   *it becomes prayer of the whole person*: Jan Woltman, "A Beginner's Journey into the Jesus Prayer," *Ministry Compass* 40, no. 1 (Spring 2011): 104.

     a sinner: Ibid.

34   *Callistus and Ignatius*: Tony Jones, *The Sacred Way* (Grand Rapids: Zondervan, 2004), 64-65.

35   *the phrase "prayer of the heart"*: Gray Henry and Jonathan Montaldo, eds., *Merton and Hesychasm: The Prayer of the Heart* (Louisville, KY: Fons Vitae, 2003), 9.

     breath in: "Lord Jesus Christ": Jones, *Sacred Way*, 65.

     three levels or degrees: Kallistos Ware, *The Orthodox Way*, rev. ed. (Yonkers, NY: St. Vladimir's Seminary Press, 1995), 123.

36   *The purpose of the Jesus Prayer*: Henry and Montaldo, *Merton and Hesychasm*, 12.

     state of imageless gazing: Ibid.

     To pray in the spirit: Ibid., 14.

37 *Only with the heart*: Antoine de Saint-Exupéry, *The Little Prince*, quoted in ibid., 5.

In the heart one can come face to face: Ibid., 6.

Calling on the name of Jesus: Irénée Hausherr, *The Name of Jesus*, trans. Charles Cummings (Kalamazoo, MI: Cistercian Publications, 1978), 119.

38 *The Christian who prays only at formal times*: Ibid., 133.

It is not enough to pray because of requirement: Ibid., 121.

3 SIMPLE PRAYER OF FAITH

42 *Prone to wander*: Robert Robinson, "Come, Thou Fount of Every Blessing," 1758, melody by John Wyeth Nettleton.

4 SIMPLE PRAYER OF FORGIVENESS

60 *The man who articulates*: Henri Nouwen, *The Wounded Healer* (New York: Doubleday, 1979), 42.

61 *forgiving the same trespass three times*: Donald A. Hagner, *Matthew 14–28*, Word Biblical Commentary 33B (Dallas, TX: Word, 1998).

5 SIMPLE PRAYER OF UNITY

73 *Prophetic ministry seeks*: Walter Brueggemann, *The Prophetic Imagination* (Philadelphia: Fortress, 1978).

6 SIMPLE PRAYER OF RESTORATION

84 *When the surrounding political kingdom's powers*: N. T. Wright, *Simply Good News: Why the Gospel Is News and What Makes It Good* (San Francisco: HarperOne, 2015).

85 *Pharisees to be portrayed as antagonists*: Walter L. Liefeld, *The Challenge of Jesus' Parables*, ed. Richard N. Longenecker (Grand Rapids: Eerdmans, 2000), 258-60.

86 *revolting members of the community*: John Nolland, *Luke 9:21–18:34*, Word Biblical Commentary 35B (Nashville: Thomas Nelson, 1993), 875.

86 *According to Luke, Jesus' inference*: Joel B. Green, *The Gospel of Luke*, New International Commentary on the New Testament (Grand Rapids: Eerdmans, 1997), 649.

The effect is a rather shocking spectacle: Ibid.

The temple had rhythms: William Hendriksen, *Exposition of the Gospel According to Luke*, New Testament Commentary (Grand Rapids: Baker Academic, 1980), 818-19.

Dennis Hamm maintains that: Dennis Hamm, "The Tamid Service in Luke-Acts: The Cultic Background Behind Luke's Theology of Worship (Luke 1:5-25; 18:9-14; 24:50-53; Acts 3:1; 10:3, 30)," *Catholic Biblical Quarterly* 65, no. 2 (April 2003): 215.

87 *great assembly of the people*: Ibid.

We are not told directly: Ibid., 224.

The Pharisee stood up and prayed: Hendriksen, *Gospel According to Luke*, 819.

One could wonder, can he only feel good: Nolland, *Luke 9:21–18:34*, 877.

88 *Instead of assuming the usual posture*: Arland J. Hultgren, *The Parables of Jesus*, The Bible in Its World (Grand Rapids: Eerdmans, 2000), 123-24.

89 *This is atonement language*: Ibid., 124.

in the state of being justified: Ibid.

the theme of justification: Robert H. Stein, *Luke*, New American Commentary 24 (Nashville: Holman Reference, 1992), 451.

91 *The audience of the story*: Robert Doran, "The Pharisee and the Tax Collector," *Catholic Biblical Quarterly* 69, no. 2 (2007): 270.

He tells stories not to inform: Eugene H. Peterson, *Tell It Slant: A Conversation on the Language of Jesus in His Stories and Prayers* (Grand Rapids: Eerdmans, 2008), 134.

7 SIMPLE WORDS TO PRAY

103 *John Climacus*: Lev Gillet and Kallistos Ware, *The Jesus Prayer* (Crestwood, NY: St. Vladimir's Seminary Press, 1987), 39-40.

Do not launch out: Ibid., 36.

104   *Most Christians for most of the centuries*: Eugene H. Peterson, "Introduction: Psalms," in *The Message: The Bible in Contemporary Language* (Colorado Springs, CO: NavPress, 2002), 910.

They show us how intimate and free: Larry Richards and Lawrence O. Richards, *The Teacher's Commentary* (Wheaton, IL: Victor Books, 1987), 325.

105   *The root word means to "lift up"*: *The Holy Bible: The Word in Life Study Bible* (Nashville, TN: Thomas Nelson, 1996).

When we read the text, we don't actually say: Roger Ellsworth, *Opening Up Psalms*, Opening Up Commentary (Leominster: Day One Publications, 2006), 11.